D0908634

Harriet Martineau

Twayne's English Authors Series

Herbert Sussman, Editor

Northeastern University

TEAS 404

HARRIET MARTINEAU
(1802–1876)
Portrait by George Richmond, 1849
Photograph courtesy of
the National Portrait Gallery, London

Harriet Martineau

By Gillian Thomas

Saint Mary's University

Twayne Publishers • *Boston*

Harriet Martineau

Gillian Thomas

Copyright © 1985 by G. K. Hall & Company
All Rights Reserved
Published by Twayne Publishers
A Division of G. K. Hall & Company
70 Lincoln Street
Boston, Massachusetts 02111

Book Production by Elizabeth Todesco

Book Design by Barbara Anderson

Printed on permanent/durable acid-free
paper and bound in the United States of
America.

Library of Congress Cataloging in Publication Data

Thomas, Gillian.
    Harriet Martineau.

    (Twayne's English authors series; TEAS 404)
    Bibliography: p. 138
    Includes index.
    1. Martineau, Harriet, 1802–1876—Criticism and
interpretation. I. Title. II. Series.
PR4984.M5Z85   1985   823′.8   84–12911
ISBN 0–8057–6894–7

Contents

About the Author

Gillian Thomas was born in Cornwall, England in 1944. After completing a B.A. and M.A. at the University of Sussex, she emigrated to Canada in 1967 to teach at the University of Victoria. She received a Ph.D. from the University of London in 1972. After teaching in Britain and California, she returned to Canada and is now an associate professor at Saint Mary's University in Halifax. Her principal scholarly interests are in nineteenth-century fiction and in the popular literature and culture of both the nineteenth and twentieth centuries. Her particular interest in this area is in the development of a mass reading public in the nineteenth century and the way in which the existence of such a public shaped popular literature. She has published numerous articles on Dickens, on children's literature, and on various aspects of nineteenth-century literature and on literature and folklore.

Preface

Modern students of nineteenth-century literature soon become familiar with the name of Harriet Martineau. She is mentioned in innumerable biographies of the major literary and political figures of her day. Participants in London literary life during the first quarter of the nineteenth century make frequent references to encounters with "Miss Martineau." Consequently, her social traits, her deafness, her intransigently held convictions, as well as her considerable influence on her contemporaries are all common knowledge to the student of nineteenth-century literature who reads the biographies and published letters of the period.

Her novels and tales, travel books, and popular didactic writings which reached such a wide readership in her own time are now barely known. The only works that the modern reader is likely to have read are the *Autobiography* (1877) and her two books of American travels, *Society in America* (1837) and *Retrospect of Western Travel* (1838). Historians are likely to be familiar with her *History of the Thirty Years' Peace* (1849) and perhaps her books on India, *British Rule in India* (1857) and *Suggestions Towards the Future Government of India* (1858).

Since Martineau was an enormously prolific writer, it is not possible within the framework of this series to comment in detail on the huge quantity of journalistic writings she produced for periodicals and newspapers or all of the ephemeral "trumpery stories" she wrote to promote her political ideas. R. K. Webb has made a significant bibliographical and critical contribution to the study of Martineau's political writings in newspapers and journals in his *Harriet Martineau: A Radical Victorian*.[1] His catalog of Martineau's leaders in the *Daily News,* available at the British Library, the Library of Congress, and the Boston Public Library, is a particularly valuable source for the historian. Many of Martineau's works are not now widely available. Intended for a wide popular audience, many of the early editions of her books were cheaply printed and bound and some of them have not survived the ravages of library use. Consequently, in some cases, the edition referred to in the body of the text is the most widely available North American edition rather than the first edition while the bibliography lists details of all first editions.

The two existing studies of Martineau and her work intended for a scholarly rather than a general audience concentrate on Martineau's historical writings and her political influence. This study is the first to evaluate her significance in the context of the nineteenth-century literary world.

Since Martineau's *Autobiography,* for all its subjectivity, remains the best source of biographical information, I have used it as the principal source for the chapter on Martineau's life. I have also tried, in that chapter, to give the reader some sense of the distortions as well as the fascinating insights presented in that work.

In the chapters on Martineau's travel writings and her popular educative literature and on her fiction I have tried to show the relationship between Martineau's writing and the development of a mass audience during the early part of the nineteenth century.

The studies of Martineau's life and work by R. K. Webb, Vera Wheatley,[2] and Valerie Kossew Pichanick,[3] although they concentrate on Martineau's historical significance, have all been of considerable value in their different ways in working on this book. I have also relied on Richard Altick's pioneering work, *The English Common Reader,*[4] in defining the nineteenth-century mass audience.

Grateful acknowledgments are due to Gwyn Pace for her assistance during the early stages of this work in obtaining some of Martineau's more obscure works and to Debbie Maxwell for her help in the final preparation of the manuscript.

Gillian Thomas

Saint Mary's University

Chronology

1802   Harriet Martineau born on 12 June in Norwich, Nor-
       folk, the sixth child and third daughter of Elizabeth Mar-
       tineau (née Rankin) and Thomas Martineau, a bomba-
       zine manufacturer.
1805   Martineau's brother James born.
1809   First reads Milton.
1811   Birth of Martineau's youngest sister, Ellen.
1813   Martineau and her sister Rachel become pupils at Mr.
       Perry's school.
1814   Early signs of deafness.
1816   Becomes deaf.
1818   Goes to stay with relatives in Bristol for fifteen months.
1820   Translates Tacitus' *Agricola*. "Female Writers of Divin-
       ity" published.
1822   Her brother James explains the "doctrine of necessity."
       Father dies.
1825   Family begins to suffer financial losses. Martineau be-
       comes engaged to John Worthington who contracts
       "brain fever" and dies.
1827   Reads Jane Marcet's *Conversations in Political Economy*.
       Begins to send articles to W. J. Fox, editor of the *Monthly
       Repository*, for critique. Final loss of the Martineau family
       fortune.
1829   Spends the winter in London unsuccessfully trying to
       place her articles with other journals than the *Repository*.
1830   Wins Unitarian essay prize. *Traditions of Palestine*.
1831   Stays in London with relatives and begins to plan political
       economy series.
1832   Moves permanently to London. *Illustrations of Political
       Economy*.

1833 Attack on Martineau by John Wilson Croker published in the *Quarterly Review*. *Poor Laws and Paupers.*

1834 Travels to America.

1836 Returns to England. Accepts commission from Saunders and Otley to write an account of her American travels. Considers editing "an Economical magazine."

1837 *Society in America.*

1838 *Deerbrook, The Guide to Service, Retrospect of Western Travel.* Attends Queen Victoria's coronation. Travels in northern England and Scotland.

1839 Becomes ill during European tour. Takes lodgings in Tynemouth.

1841 *The Hour and the Man, The Playfellow.*

1843 Refuses a government pension.

1844 Advised to try mesmeric cure and begins treatments. *Life in the Sickroom.*

1845 Recovers health and goes into lodgings at Windermere. *Letters on Mesmerism.* Asks friends to destroy her letters. First meeting with Henry Atkinson.

1846 Moves into The Knoll at Ambleside. Travels to Egypt.

1848 *Eastern Life, Past and Present.* Death of Martineau's mother.

1849 *History of the Peace, Household Education.* Meets Charlotte Brontë.

1850 Invited by Dickens to contribute to *Household Words.*

1851 *Letters on the Laws of Man's Nature and Development.* James Martineau attacks the book in the *Prospective Review.*

1852 Begins writing leader columns for the *Daily News.*

1853 *The Positive Philosophy of Auguste Comte.*

1854 Becomes ill and consults London physicians. Begins her autobiography, believing it to be her final work.

1857 *British Rule in India.*

1861 *Health, Husbandry and Handicraft.*

1864 Martineau's niece, Maria, dies.

1869   *Biographical Sketches.*

1876   Martineau dies on 27 June.

1877   Posthumous publication of *Harriet Martineau's Autobiography.*

Chapter One

A "Somewhat Remarkable" Life

Family and Childhood

In her *Autobiography,* Harriet Martineau records that her life was one which "began with winter" and burst forth into summer "without any interval of spring."[1] Her account of herself as a suffering and sensitive child is one which makes every effort to be fair to her family but which nonetheless gives the impression of a dismally unyielding system of child rearing.

The Martineaus' ancestors had been Huguenots who had emigrated to England from France in the late sixteenth century to escape the religious persecution that followed the revocation of the Edict of Nantes in 1686. The traditional family vocation had been medicine until Harriet's father became a textile manufacturer specializing in dress materials. Middle-class Norwich in the early nineteenth century was regarded as culturally sophisticated for a provincial town, and it is evident that the eight Martineau children, of whom Harriet was the sixth, were the beneficiaries of an attitude that favored both male and female children receiving an academic education.

Although the intellectual atmosphere in the Martineau home may have been a stimulating one, the emotional climate was repressive. The attitude taken toward all children was stern and unbending. Martineau describes it in her *Autobiography* as "the 'taking down' system" (1:20), and it is evident that this resulted in an early repression of spontaneous feeling and expression. She recounts an anecdote of herself as a five year old suffering from an unbearable earache and shutting herself in a room at the top of the house to howl with pain. Eventually she creeps into a dark corner of the room where the rest of the family is sitting: "Presently my mother called to me, and asked what I

was doing there. Then I burst out,—that my ear ached so I
did not know *what* to do! Then she and my father both called
me tenderly, and she took me on her lap, and laid the ear on
her warm bosom. I was afraid of spoiling her starched muslin
handkerchief with the tears which *would* come; but I was very
happy, and wished that I need never move again" (1:21). It
is startling to find parental tenderness so rare that such an incident is intensely memorable for the child, so we are not surprised
to learn that, throughout her early childhood, Martineau had
no confidence that her parents really loved her. She describes
herself as "an intolerable child"(1:21), but suggests that this
was directly attributable to a want of tenderness in those who
cared for her:

I really think, if I had once conceived that any body cared for me,
nearly all the sins and sorrows of my anxious childhood would have
been spared me; and I remember well that it was Ann Turner who
first conveyed the cheering truth to me. She asked me why my mother
sat sewing so diligently for us children, and sat up at night to mend
my stockings, if she did not care for me; and I was convinced at
once;—only too happy to believe it, and being unable to resist such
evidence as the stocking-mending at night, when we children were
asleep. (1:29)

Although upbringing of this kind seems unusually cruel to
the modern reader, the childhood accounts of many of Martineau's contemporaries are often strikingly similar. Charlotte
Brontë remarked that she believed when she read *Household
Education* (1849), which drew heavily on Martineau's own childhood, that "It was like meeting her own fetch,—so precisely
were the fears and miseries there described the same as her
own, told or not told in 'Jane Eyre.'" Similarly, when Harriet
Martineau first read *Jane Eyre* in 1837 before Charlotte Brontë
was known to be the author, she became "convinced that it
was by some friend of my own, who had portions of my childhood experience in his or her mind" (1:324).

The emotional austerity of Martineau's childhood was, like
Charlotte Brontë's own, further blighted by poor health. Like
most middle-class children of the time, she was sent to a wet
nurse for the first phase of babyhood, but this resulted in her

case in near-starvation since "the wetnurse being very poor [was] holding on to her good place after the milk was going or gone"(1:10). This state of semistarvation was not discovered until the child was nearly three months old. She was also, evidently, a nervous child plagued with night fears, which must have been the more intolerable in the absence of parental reassurance.

Predictably, her first refuge from the excessive severity of her home was in religious belief. Under the influence of a later nurse, "a Methodist or melancholy Calvinist of some sort," she became, at the age of two or three, "the absurdest little preacher of my years . . . that ever was. I used to nod my head emphatically, and say 'Never ky for tyfles:' 'Dooty fust, and pleasure afterwards,' and so forth: and I sometimes got the courage to edge up to strangers, and ask them to give me—'a maxim'" (1:12). Fortunately, her parents did not share the severe Calvinism of her nurse. As Unitarians, their interpretation of Scriptures was a liberal one and, unlike many nineteenth-century middle-class children, Martineau was not terrorized with threats of Hell. Although she would soon become dissatisfied with "the shallow scholarship of the Unitarians [which] made its own choice about what to receive and what to reject, without perceiving that such a process was wholly incompatible with the conception of the Scriptures being the record of a divine revelation at all" (1:38), she readily admitted the benefits of a religious belief that permitted interpretation, discussion, and enquiry rather than being rigidly bound in dogma. At the age of eleven, she became deeply troubled by the question of how a bountiful and powerful deity could permit suffering and evil. Her brother James, "then my oracle," suggested that an answer might lie in the "necessarian" doctrine of the existence of certain "eternal and irreversible laws, working in every department of the universe, without any interference from any random will, human or divine" (1:111). At the time, she readily incorporated the necessarian view into a conventional Unitarian Christian framework but, to her brother James's later chagrin, necessarianism became the cornerstone of her eventual rejection of Christianity.

As we might deduce from this early preoccupation with religious and philosophical questions, Martineau was, at least by modern standards, an intellectually precocious child. At the age

of seven she accidentally discovered a copy of *Paradise Lost:*
"The first thing I saw was 'Argument' which I took to mean
a dispute, and supposed to be stupid enough: but there was
something about Satan cleaving Chaos, which made me turn
to the poetry; and my mental destiny was fixed for the next
seven years." Milton's verse became so vividly imprinted on
the child's imagination that "when my curtains were drawn back
in the morning, descriptions of heavenly light rushed into my
memory" (1:42). A few years later, her greatest solace was
reading Shakespeare by firelight as soon as supper was over.

By the time she was fourteen, she had already developed
an active interest in what was to become a lifelong preoccupation: "political economy"—the economic and social theory originally formulated by David Ricardo and Adam Smith among
others and later adopted as the core of utilitarian philosophy.
The Martineau family newspaper was the *Globe* which "without
ever mentioning Political Economy . . . taught it, and viewed
public affairs in its light" (1:70), but even before becoming
an avid newspaper reader, she was particularly attracted to the
section of the school geography book that dealt with economic
matters. At this period, Malthus's theory of population was
widely discussed, although, as Martineau points out, few people
had actually read his book. When Martineau eventually met
Malthus many years later, she told him, to his considerable
amusement, that she had become "sick of his name" before
she was fifteen (1:71).

Despite this sort of intellectual precocity by which the young
Harriet Martineau became "a political economist without knowing it, and, at the same time, a sort of walking concordance
of Milton and Shakespeare" (1:71–72), her early intellectual
development took place within formidable constraints. Even in
the Martineau family where the academic education of girls as
well as boys was encouraged, there was some sense that it was
improper for a young woman to study with real commitment,
"and especially with pen in hand" (1:100). Thus, Martineau's
first studies were carried out at the fringes of the day, either
in the early morning or late at night when she was not required
to fulfill her customary duties of making her own clothes or
those of the rest of the family. This established a pattern of
reading and writing early and late and sleeping for only a few
hours each night which was to last the rest of her life.

At this period, she devoted considerable attention to translating from the Latin: "and a good preparation it proved for the subsequent work of my life. Now, it was meeting James at seven in the morning to read Lowth's Prelections in the Latin, after having been busy since five about something else, in my own room. Now it was translating Tacitus, in order to try what was the utmost compression of style that I could attain" (1:101). The self-imposed rigor of her working hours and her concentration on a simple and compressed rather than a highly mannered style undoubtedly laid the foundation for a pattern of work that would enable her to become one of the most popular and prolific writers of her day.

Martineau's deafness seems to have developed gradually and almost imperceptibly from the age of twelve. She recalls experiencing some difficulty hearing the teacher in the large schoolroom at Mr. Perry's school when she was about twelve years old, but her deafness did not become fully apparent till she was fifteen. Evidently, her family's attitude compounded the difficulty she faced in acclimatizing herself to almost total deafness. At first they insisted that she was not deaf at all, but merely inattentive, "and ever (while my heart was breaking) they told me that 'none are so deaf as those that won't hear' " (1:76). Martineau's distress at the onset of deafness was increased by her memories of the family's irritation at receiving a deaf visitor: "if she came up the steps, it grew into lamentation. 'What *shall* we do?' 'We shall be as hoarse as ravens all day' " (1:77). She developed a real terror of being "dreaded and disliked" in a similar manner until her eldest brother advised her on the matter. He had been out to dine and one of the guests had been an elderly Miss N. who had irritated her companions by trying to compensate for her deafness by asking for every remark at the table to be repeated: "My brother told me, with tenderness in his voice, that he thought of me while blushing, as every body present did, for Miss N——; and that he hoped that if ever I should grow as deaf as she, I should never be seen making myself so irksome and absurd. This helped me to a resolution which I made and never broke,—never to ask what was said" (1:74). Martineau evidently accepted this somewhat harsh lesson with gratitude and formulated a firm resolve never to ask anyone to repeat remarks made to the company at large. This specific resolution was one aspect of Martineau's deliberate effort at

this stage to take "my temper in hand,—in this way. I was young
enough for vows,—was, indeed, at the very age of vows;—and
I made a vow of patience about this infirmity;—that I would
smile in every moment of anguish from it; and that I would
never lose temper at any consequences from it" (1:76–77). The
self-mastery she achieved as a result of this vow gave her the
view in the final phase of her life that "this same deafness is
about the best thing that ever happened to me" (1:78). As
her deafness was developing, however, it is plain, from her
assessment in the *Autobiography* and through her hard-won advice in "Letter to the Deaf" (1834), that the period was one
of profound and lonely suffering.

Her deafness, nervousness, and poor health might have been
easier to bear if she had been treated with a little more tenderness at home. Instead, her mother, who evidently preferred
Harriet's older sister, Rachel, seems to have allowed Rachel
to persistently snub the younger child. One memorable day,
in the course of a family argument, Harriet challenged her
mother with continually favoring Rachel at her expense. It was
a moment of enormous tension:

My hands were clammy and tremulous; my fingers stuck to each other;
my eyes were dim, and there was a roaring in my ears. . . . My
mother laid down her work, and said, 'Harriet, I am more displeased
with you to-night than ever I have been in your life.' Thought I, 'I
don't care: I have got it out, and it is all true.' 'Go and say your
prayers.' Thought I,—'No, I shan't,' And I did not: and that was
the only night from my infancy to mature womanhood that I did
not pray. I detected misgiving in my mother's forced manner and I
triumphed. If the right was on my side (as I entirely believed) the
power was on hers; and what the next morning was to be I could
not conceive. I slept little and went down sick with dread. Not a
word was said, however, then or ever, of the scene of the preceding
night; but henceforth, a most scrupulous impartiality between Rachel
and me was shown. (1:86)

Remarkably, by the time she reached her late teens, Martineau
had largely mastered her own complex and difficult temperament
through her courageous confrontation of her deafness and had
begun to train herself in the skills that would be invaluable in
her life as a writer. The struggle that would remain with her

in one form or another until the final phases of her life was her recurring conflict with members of her family about the direction her life and thought should take.

Early Struggles

Martineau's first attempt at authorship was the result of a pact with her brother James who suggested that she should write an article for submission to the Unitarian periodical the *Monthly Repository* in order to occupy herself when he returned to college. She wrote a piece on "Female Writers of Practical Divinity," "feeling mightily like a fool all the time," and submitted it under the pseudonym "V." At the end of the month, her oldest brother was reading the *Repository* aloud to her and exclaimed with admiration at the piece "V of Norwich." He was surprised and puzzled by her reluctance to concur with his praise and pursued the topic till she confusedly burst out, "I never could baffle any body. The truth is that paper is mine." He carefully read the rest of the article in silence, "He then laid his hand on my shoulder, and said gravely (calling me 'dear' for the first time) 'Now, dear, leave it to other women to make shirts and darn stockings; and do you devote yourself to this.' I went home in sort of a dream, so that the squares of the pavement seemed to float before my eyes. That evening made me an authoress" (1:120).

Two apparently unconnected events followed this first attempt at authorship and served indirectly to determine her future career. During Martineau's early twenties her family's financial fortunes were going into a steady decline, and at this period she agreed to marry John Worthington whose confidence in his prospects as a suitor seems to have been encouraged by the decline in the Martineau family's fortunes. The engagement was evidently a reluctant one on Martineau's part and the unhappy situation was resolved when Worthington became insane and died as a result of a "brain-fever"—the nineteenth-century catchall term for any serious physical illness accompanied by psychological symptoms. Reflecting on the episode in the final phases of her life, Martineau considered herself very fortunate not to have married since she regarded both her temperament and her vocation as best suited to living alone.

The family investments disintegrated entirely in 1829 leaving Martineau "destitute;—that is to say, with precisely one shilling in my purse" (1:141). Even at the time, Martineau regarded the family's "misfortune" as a lucky turn of events in that it conferred a new freedom:

for we had lost our gentility. Many and many a time since have we said that, but for that loss of money, we might have lived on in the ordinary provincial method of ladies with small means, sewing, and economizing, and growing narrower every year; whereas, by being thrown, while it was yet time, on our own resources, we have worked hard and usefully, won friends, reputation and independence, seen the world abundantly, abroad and at home, and, in short, have truly lived instead of vegetated. (1:142)

Since her deafness ruled out the possibility of the traditional resort of "governessing," Martineau placed her main immediate hope in earning enough to support herself by means of working at fancy needlework during the daylight hours while spending every night writing. She received a commission from W. J. Fox, the new editor of the *Monthly Repository,* to review books for the annual stipend of fifteen pounds which was followed by Fox's request that she send to him "two or three tales, such as his 'best readers' would not pass by" (1:145). Encouraged by this beginning, she went to London in the hope of making a start on a literary career; but without "literary acquaintance or connection whatever I could not get anything that I wrote looked at; so that every thing went into the 'Repository' at last" (1:146). Although her stay in London yielded no firm commissions, she had several offers of work undertaking "proof-correcting and other literary drudgery" and she felt confident that she could support herself with this work "while leaving time for literary effort on my own account" (1:148–49).

To her enormous disappointment, she received "peremptory orders" from her mother to return home. In later life, she was astonished that she should have, at the age of twenty-seven, complied so readily with such an unreasonable and impractical demand. Apparently her mother had been convinced by relatives that her daughter would do better, "to pursue,—not literature but needlework" (1:148–49).

Although Martineau may have viewed her capitulation to her mother's views incredulously from her later perspective as an established author, it must have seemed less surprising at the time. There was little to suggest that a career as a writer was inevitable. Unlike many writers whose careers develop from a childhood of inveterate and compulsive scribbling, Martineau's first attempts at writing were extremely timid, sustained mainly by her brother's encouragement. Later, her determination to make her living by writing was galvanized largely by the family's loss of fortune, and at such a time of profound anxiety about the future it is not so surprising to find her open to the suggestion that even needlework might offer a more secure income than authorship.

On her return to Norwich, she learned of the small essay prize being offered by the *Repository,* "by which Unitarianism was to be presented to the notice of Catholics, Jews and Mohammedans" (1:150). Despite the fairly small amount of prize money being offered, she decided to submit an entry for each of the three categories. She worked at these and other essays and tales during every waking hour that was not spent in making and mending clothes or reading aloud to her mother and aunt. After a year of this effort, her mother finally realized "the necessity of my being a good deal in London" and consented "to spare me for three months in the spring of every year" (1:154). On her return to London, Martineau learned that her essays for the Unitarian contest had won all three prizes and she regarded the news as an indication that "authorship was my legitimate career" (1:156).

Before long she had formulated a plan for a series of tales that would illustrate the basic principles of political economy. She had read Jane Marcet's didactic, *Conversations on Political Economy,* [2] and thought that she might do something similar showing the workings of "the principles of the whole science . . . in selected passages of social life" (1:138). She visited publisher after publisher with the proposal and was rejected each time on the grounds that the public was too preoccupied with the Reform Bill and the cholera epidemic to have any interest in such a series. Eventually, Fox's brother Charles, who was a bookseller rather than a publisher, made her an offer which required her to find five hundred subscribers to the work. The search for subscribers was as humiliating as the earlier rejections by publishers had been. Among the various snubs she received was a letter from a cousin, "enclosing two sovereigns, and a lecture against my rashness and presumption in supposing that I was adequate to such a work as authorship, and offering the enclosed sum as his mite towards the subscription; but recommending rather a family subscription which might eke out my earnings by my needle" (1:168).

Even under his own well-protected terms, Charles Fox began to take fright at the venture and insisted that the work would have to sell a thousand copies in the first two weeks or else he would withdraw from the agreement. Profoundly discouraged, Martineau set out to return to the house of the relatives with whom she was staying: "I could not afford to ride . . . but, weary already, I now felt almost too ill to walk at all. On the road, not far from Shoreditch, I became too giddy to stand without support; and I leaned over some dirty palings, pretending to look at a cabbage bed, but saying to myself, as I stood with closed eyes, 'My book will do yet' " (1:170). That evening, she sat down to write the preface to the *Illustrations of Political Economy* (1832).

The sales of the series had a slow start until Martineau, at her mother's suggestion, sent a circular to all members of Parliament describing the work. Sales snowballed and the work was generally well-received by the press.

From February of 1832, Martineau's life became largely free of "pecuniary care" although the strain on her health during the preceding two years had been enormous. The success of the series compelled her to move to London to pursue her literary interests, and she began by taking lodgings in Conduit Street until the autumn of 1833 when she moved into the house in Fludyer Street, Westminster, where she lived till the serious breakdown of her health in 1839. For the time, however, her life was entering into a sunny period, "bursting forth without any interval of spring" (1:180).

Fame

The modern reader cannot help but find it astonishing that the basis of Harriet Martineau's early fame rested on her *Illustra-*

tions of Political Economy. The tiny volumes with their often contrived sequences of events and forced didactic dialogue now have an unconsciously comic quality for modern readers not used to unabashed didactic writing.

In the 1830s public debate about political and economic matters was taking place, not only among the educated, wealthy, and enfranchised but also among the growing population of urban artisans. The steady drift of manual workers to the cities necessitated by the industrial revolution was creating not only a sense of political solidarity among working people, but opportunities for debate that life in small rural centers could rarely offer. In this ferment of social and political ideas the rule-of-thumb simplistic interpretation of social and economic phenomena which Martineau provided may well have seemed to many of her readers to provide a safe formula for political policymaking. In any event, the *Illustrations* were enormously popular, and Martineau was soon beset by individuals or groups who wanted her to promote their views within the format of the series:

It was, in fact, rather ridiculous to see the onset on my acquaintances made by riders of hobbies. One acquaintance of mine told me, as I was going to his house to dinner, that three gentlemen had been at his office that morning;—one beseeching him to get me to write a number on the navigable rivers of Ireland; a second on (I think) the Hamiltonian (or other) system of Education; and a third, who was confident that the welfare of the nation depended on it, on the encouragement of flaxgrowing in the interior of Guiana. (1:231)

The series was also a controversial one. The sixth in the series, "Weal and Woe in Garveloch," for example, dealt with Malthusian principles, and Martineau was aware that many would regard the subject as an improper one. She felt anxious while writing the tale: "the perspiration many a time streamed down my face, though I knew there was not a line in it which might not be read aloud in any family" (1:200). Even before she dealt with the population question in her series, she had been pestered by people who had wanted to know how she intended to treat the issue. She handled interference of this sort quite calmly, indicating that she regarded it as "a strictly philosophical question" offering no difficulty to those who approached it as such: "If any other should come whispering to me what I need not listen to, I shall shift my trumpet, and take up my knitting" (1:202).

Other topics covered in the series proved similarly controversial. At first the tales appealed to reactionary opinion in Britain and Europe, but later the populist nature of her conservatism offended her early supporters. Mrs. Marcet was excited when the initial numbers of the series were enthusiastically supported by several European monarchs but she was distressed when Martineau offended the French king by "writing about Egalité." The French king was not the only ruler to withdraw support. The Russian czar and Austrian emperor both ordered all copies of the series to be burned and Martineau was prohibited from entering either Russia or the Austrian Empire. Martineau was, typically, unmoved by this display of royal disfavor, declaring that she had written the series "with a view to the people . . . and the crowned heads must, for once, take their chance for their feelings" (1:236).

The success of the series brought her into the center of the attention of literary London. She found herself "lionized" at evening parties, but made a deliberate effort to resist being paraded by competitive hostesses. She regarded the custom of lionizing literary figures in this manner as one likely to prove detrimental to the writer. The real danger, as she saw it, was that the "lion" began to believe that books were influential in the world at large, whereas in reality to most people books, other than cheap sensational works, were of little or no consequence.

While she might manage to avoid some of the damaging process of being lionized, it was impossible to avoid deliberate attacks on her reputation. The *Quarterly Review*'s fame for brutal attacks has survived because of Byron's famous rhyme: "Who killed John Keats? / 'I,' says the Quarterly, / So savage and Tartarly; / ' 'Twas one of my feats.' "[3] John Wilson Croker told his acquaintances at a dinner party that he expected to lose his government pension and intended to start to earn his living by writing, beginning "by tomahawking Miss Martineau in the Quarterly" (1:206). Even before Croker's review was published, rumors about the nature of the piece began to circulate. John Gibson Lockhart, Croker's collaborator in the venture, made a hasty attempt to meet Martineau socially, knowing that the opportunity would never arise again after the review was published. A relative of Lockhart's, who had met Martineau, urged him either to suppress or modify the attack. Evidently Lockhart was sufficiently edgy about the matter to go to the printers at the last moment to cut out "all the worst passages" of the review, though, as Martineau herself acidly remarks, it is hard to imagine how the original could have been more abusive than the final version.

The review, as published, is a strange document. It makes some legitimate criticisms of the simplistic quality of the political views propounded in the series, but it relies for the most part on a tone of hysterical outrage that "unfeminine and mischievous doctrines on the principles of social welfare"[4] should be promulgated by a woman, "a *female Malthusian. A woman* who thinks child-bearing a *crime against society!* An *unmarried woman* who declares against *marriage!!*"[5] Though her family and friends were anxious about how Martineau would react, she seems to have borne her "first trial in the shape of hostile reviewing" with equanimity, finding herself "Unharmed, and somewhat enlightened and strengthened" (1:206).

Martineau's sudden prominence in literary London provided her with an opportunity to meet some of the writers who had been mythic figures when she was growing up in Norwich. Sydney Smith, Bulwer Lytton, and the poet Thomas Campbell were all rapidly reduced in her eyes from monumental stature to ordinary human figures beset with ordinary vanities and absurdities. No sycophant, Martineau was less impressed by the fame of other writers than by the manner in which they accepted the capricious nature of literary popularity. She very much admired Johanna Baillie whose reputation had long since sunk into obscurity, because she bore the "bitter trial" of a long-eclipsed fame with such cheerfulness and serenity. In describing the literary giants of the day, Martineau has a fine sense of anecdote which she would later develop to good advantage in the essays on her contemporaries, which were eventually published as *Biographical Sketches* (1869). She is at her best when describing those of whom she was personally fond. She shows us, for example, the irascible Carlyle forever discontented with the noise and interruptions of Chelsea. He went looking for another house, "with three maps of Great Britain and two of the World in his pocket, to explore the area within twenty miles of London" (1:378).

Despite the fact that she evidently enjoyed the social aspect of her literary fame, it was not without its irritations. She was plagued by the attentions of admirers who would filch her pen or make a sketch of her for a souvenir. Aspiring writers would demand her opinion on their work or her advice on how to conduct their lives: "One young clergyman I remember who felt that he was made for immortality in the line of Shakesperian tragedy; but he wanted my opinion as to whether he should begin in that way at once, or try something else; and especially, whether or not I should advise him to drink beer" (1:409).

Attention of this sort was time-consuming and sometimes irritating, but much more problematical were the reactions of Martineau's mother to her daughter's newfound fame. Although Martineau is circumspect in her description, it seems clear that her mother was jealous of the popular interest her daughter's work had aroused. Particularly, she was discontented with the relatively humble Fludyer Street house and urged living "in some sort of style,—to have a larger house in a better street, and lay out our mode of living for the society in which I was moving" (1:249). Martineau was aware that a grander domestic style would be a drain on her income and that such a change might press her into writing for strictly financial motives. She remained firm, "It was my fixed resolution never to mortgage my brains" (1:249). She was aware that the pace at which she had to write the political economy series had subjected her to enormous strain and was thoroughly alarmed at the idea of "assuming a position which could be maintained only by excessive toil" (1:250). The conflict was not finally resolved until 1839 when her illness rendered either the maintenance of a London household or earning her living by writing out of the question for several years.

In many respects the continual eruptions of conflict between Martineau and her mother recall the similar relationship between Florence Nightingale and her mother and sister. Nightingale's mother constantly pressed her daughter to use her fame after she returned from the Crimea to extend and upgrade her social circle. Indeed, Cecil Woodham-Smith, in her biography

of Florence Nightingale,[6] has suggested that Nightingale's prolonged invalidism was, in fact, a device through which she could
avoid social demands and continue with her work. It is tempting
to speculate that Martineau's years of retirement at Tynemouth
may have been precipitated in part by similar unconscious motives, but her own account of her symptoms does not immediately suggest such an interpretation. However, for both
Martineau and Florence Nightingale, the social role of invalid,
whether or not it was entirely necessary from a physiological
point of view, permitted a withdrawal from trivial or irritating
social commitments. The two women's careers have interesting
parallels in this and several other respects, particularly their
political influence. It is unfortunate that their extensive correspondence did not survive Martineau's request to her associates
that her letters be destroyed.

Respite from two and a half years of hectic work and a busy
social life came with Martineau's trip to America, planned, in
part, simply to act as an antidote to the intense effort and preoccupation of her London life. However, the choice of destination
was a significant one. She had already tested her theories of
political economy against the examples of British social institutions she saw around her, and it was logical to want firsthand
experience of a country whose institutions had been deliberately
designed in contrast to those of the Old World. She finished
the final tale of the political economy series only one day before
she was due to leave for Liverpool on the first leg of her journey.
Something of her overwrought state of mind can be deduced
by her sensations on taking a walk in St. James Park immediately
after concluding the final tale: "It felt very like flying. The
grass under foot, the sky overhead, the trees round about were
wholly different from what they had ever appeared before"
(1:226–27). She had previously agreed to a writing assignment
under the title "How to Observe," and, despite her weariness,
she fulfilled the agreement while on her voyage to America.
The routine quality of the result, *How to Observe Morals and
Manners* (1838), shows all too clearly the effects of the strain
of the preceding two years' work. Fortunately Martineau herself
recognized that she was in need of a complete break from literary
effort and, apart from her unpublished journal, wrote nothing
during her American travels.

The account of her journey provided in *Society in America*

and in *Retrospect of Western Travel* overlaps considerably with
the *Autobiography*. While the account in the latter is naturally
briefer, it concentrates more exclusively on her experiences in
relation to the politics of slavery and the abolitionists and is
more frank about the effects of her public abolitionist stand
on her social reception. She gives an amusing account of how
some social "lion-hunters" reneged on their invitations to her
after she had made a public statement at an abolitionist meeting
and then tried to recoup their social losses when it appeared
that her public stand had not, after all, resulted in her being
shunned. In a more serious vein, she is more explicit in the
Autobiography about the threats to her personal safety that resulted from her antislavery stance, and it is evident that she
and her American companions regarded the various threats to
lynch her as very credible. For part of the journey, the possibility
of such an attack was a daily reality, "I believe that there was
scarcely a morning during those three months when it was not
my first thought on waking whether I should be alive at night"
(2:55). Characteristically, Martineau coolly evaluates such a prospect in terms of its likely effect on bringing slavery to an end
and somewhat regrets that she did not become the victim of a
lynching, since she suspected that the murder of a British subject
might have more effective repercussions "than followed the
slaughter of native Abolitionists" (2:56). Martineau's abolitionist convictions combined with her attraction to the political institutions of America made her seriously consider the prospect
of eventually settling in the New World, but these tentative
plans were effectively brought to an end by the intervention
of her long illness.

   On her return from America, Martineau was, predictably
enough, beset with offers from publishers anxious to publish
her account of her travels. While some might have found such
attention flattering, Martineau seems to have felt that the jockey-
ing between rival publishers was distasteful. She cut short the
negotiations by offering the manuscript to Saunders and Otley,
whom she considered reputable and reliable, rather than selling
to the highest bidder.

   The pattern of her life at this time gave every indication of
resembling the busy literary and social existence she had led
in London before her American travels. She was invited to edit

"an Economical magazine" and debated agonizingly with herself whether "the toil and bondage" of editorship would be compensated by the opportunity "of showing what a periodical with a perfect temper may be" as well as the chance of "setting women forward at one with the rank of men of business" (2:110). Her London friends urged acceptance of the offer, but she continued to procrastinate until she had received a letter from her brother. James was emphatically opposed to the scheme, and Harriet immediately wrote to the publisher to refuse the offer. We might interpret this decision as a further example of Martineau's susceptibility to being browbeaten by her family, but it seems more likely that she used James's advice to support her own reluctance to tether herself to a lengthy and constraining literary task.

There were also two schemes for novels at the back of her mind. She had accidentally come upon an article on the Haitian leader, Touissant L'Ouverture, in the *Quarterly Review* and fancied that his life would make a worthwhile subject for a novel. The friend to whom she confided the idea discouraged her from proceeding, and what became *The Hour and the Man* (1841) was thus deferred for several years. She turned instead to a domestic subject. The idea, derived from a family she knew slightly, was of a man deeply in love with one woman who is persuaded that he has compromised her sister and thus feels that he is required to marry a woman whom he does not love. The resulting novel, *Deerbrook* (1839), was only moderately successful mainly because of the social class of the characters. The large middle class which was essentially the audience of nineteenth-century novels enjoyed reading about crime or low life in the "Newgate" novel or in *Oliver Twist* and had a taste for reading about the real or imagined lives of the wealthy and aristocratic; it had not yet developed a taste for reading about itself. *Deerbrook* missed becoming a major popular success, less because of its faults as a work of fiction, as because it failed to provide the account of upper-class manners that a socially aspiring middle class craved. Martineau was amused by the disdain expressed for the novel's characters: "It was droll to hear the daughters of dissenting ministers and manufacturers express disgust that the heroine came from Birmingham, and that the hero was a surgeon" (2:115).

In the midst of writing *Deerbrook* she was persuaded to spend part of the fall of 1838 traveling in the north of England and in Scotland. She recognized that she was becoming tired and overstrained, but was eventually persuaded to travel, less for the sake of her health than because Charles Knight wanted her to provide topographical notes for his edition of Shakespeare. The Scottish tour could supply the necessary background for *Macbeth* and her tour of Italy the following year could provide the notes for the Italian plays. The notion of topographical notes, when, in all probability, Shakespeare never visited either region, is an odd one by the standards of modern literary scholarship but was considered a worthwhile adjunct to an edition of the time. In any event, it was an enjoyable task and Martineau thought it "almost as pleasant work as any I ever had to do" (2:135).

Invalid Life

Domestic difficulties continued to mount. During her northern travels she was suddenly called back to Newcastle for a family emergency. Her mother continued to feel resentful about Martineau's social position but was also fast becoming blind and was reluctant to acknowledge the fact. While she bore her blindness with patience, her "natural irritability found vent in other directions" (2:150) and worryingly, she persisted in going out alone despite her failing sight.

Although she makes little of its emotional impact, Martineau suffered a further personal loss at this time. During her American travels she had met a young slave girl, Ailsie, whose mistress died and left her "to be a most embarrassing charge" to the liberally minded widower. He had written to Martineau and they had formed an agreement that she would adopt the child. It is evident that Martineau eagerly anticipated freeing Ailsie from slave-labor:

I intended first to train her as my little maid, and have her attend a school near, so that I might ascertain what she was most fit for. All this winter, we were in daily expectation of her arrival. Her little bed awaited her in my room; and we had arranged about having her vaccinated at once, and clothed like English children, instead of having her brilliant eyes and beautiful mulatto face surmounted by the yellow turban which became her so well. (2:143)

Ailsie failed to appear, and eventually Martineau received a distraught letter from her American friend. His debts had prevented him from freeing Ailsie and she had been reclaimed by his mother-in-law.

Valerie Kossew Pichanick[7] is critical of Martineau's proposed scheme of training Ailsie as a maid, suggesting that this was the result of unacknowledged racial prejudice. By modern standards, such a scheme as Martineau proposed is, of course, a patronizing one, but the social history, the fiction, and the biography of the nineteenth century illustrates in innumerable cases that the distinction between adopting a child and indenturing a servant was often an extremely cloudy one for the Victorian middle class. There are many cases of well-off families "adopting" a child from an orphanage or from a street-urchin life and installing the child in the family as a more or less favored servant. To charge that Martineau was acting hypocritically in this case is to suggest that it was possible for her to share attitudes which have only begun to exist decades after her death. At any rate, the sudden abandonment of the eagerly anticipated scheme was almost certainly a further blow to Martineau's failing health.

Although some of her friends had predicted that she was on the verge of illness, the onset of a serious complaint was itself quite sudden. In the midst of her European tour, while staying in Venice, her collapse "broke up all our plans" and she was brought home and placed under the care of her brother-in-law, the physician Thomas Greenhow.

Because of the unusual circumstances of her recovery and the way in which Greenhow later publicized the precise character of her symptoms, the nature of Martineau's illness is less shrouded in mystery than those of other nineteenth-century figures, such as Darwin or Elizabeth Barrett, who went through long periods of invalidism. She seems to have suffered from a uterine tumour, which caused considerable pain through pressure on other organs. She also seems to have had a prolapsed uterus, which was probably the source of chronic cystitis. Martineau was frank in her description of her symptoms in her letter

to Thomas Greenhow and, unlike many Victorian women, was
neither coy nor prudish about internal examination. The treatment which Greenhow prescribed was leeching, combined with
opiates for the pain, in addition to the usual panacea that was
administered to ailing Victorian women: "rest."

Clearly, life in London made no provision for the rest her
physician prescribed, and Martineau decided to go into lodgings
at Tynemouth which was in easy reach of her doctor. Her family
was skeptical about whether she could tolerate the solitude and
monotony of a Tynemouth sickroom after the constant excitement of London, but she insisted on her experiment.

Martineau's assessment of her experiences as an invalid is
recorded in *Life in the Sickroom* (1844) to which she refers in
her *Autobiography* as one of her most deeply felt works. She
used the book as a medium for confiding her thoughts on how
a prolonged illness affects the sufferer's world view and found
immense relief in imparting the confidence. The book was, for
this reason, astonishingly easy to write: "I never wrote anything
so fast as that book. It went off like sleep. I was hardly conscious
of the act, while writing or afterwards,—so strong was the need
to speak" (2:170). Framed as advice to "some fellow sufferer,"
the book is really a meditation on the psychological effects of
physical illness. She warns against the dangers of loss of perspective consequent on the strictures of sickroom life, which turns
past "trifling errors" into obsessions, and recommends that the
invalid take pains to retain a broad inclusive view of the world,
thus turning the sickroom into a place of moral education. For
similar reasons, she warns against the invalid keeping a diary
since it can serve as the source of excessive subjectivity and
morbidity.

Her own sickroom experience was somewhat less solitary than
Life in the Sickroom might suggest. She had many visitors, though
she was careful to restrict visiting times to those periods when
the opiates were providing relief from pain. Her conversations
with her Tynemouth visitors evidently had a quieter, more re-
flective quality than had been possible in the hectic pace of
London literary life:

During many a summer evening, while I lay on my window-couch,
and my guest of the day sat beside me, overlooking the purple sea,

or watching for the moon to rise up from it, like a planet growing
into a sun, things were said, high and deep, which are fixed in my
memory now, like stars in a dark firmament. Now a philosopher,
now a poet, now a moralist, opened to me speculation, vision, or
conviction; and numerous as all the speculations, visions and convictions together, were the doubts confided to my meditation . . . .
(2:187–88)

Even the somewhat secluded nature of her life in her Tynemouth sickroom did not remove her from public attention. At
this time, because of her inevitably rather straitened financial
circumstances, she was offered a government pension. She twice
refused the offer because she feared that accepting a pension
would inhibit her from writing freely on political issues. Her
refusal was regarded by many as a form of false pride. Lord
Brougham was most notably irate on the subject: " 'Harriet
Martineau! I hate her!' Being asked why, he replied, 'I hate a
woman who has opinions, She has refused a pension,—making
herself out to be better than other people!' " (2:176–77).

Mesmeric Cure

The "passive period" of Martineau's long illness had certainly
not been without controversy. Her refusal of a government
pension had offended some and her insistence that her family
and friends destroy her correspondence to prevent posthumous
publication had irritated others. Her brother James's refusal
to comply with her request to destroy the letters resulted in a
rapid cooling of their relationship. The circumstances of her
cure, however, were even more dramatic in creating a serious
rift between Harriet and some members of her family.

During the middle period of her Tynemouth sojourn she
had received a letter from Bulwer Lytton enthusiastically recommending a mesmeric practitioner in Paris. She was receptive
to the notion but was too ill to travel. She was also aware that
her family would be opposed to treatment that carried strong
associations of quackery and chicanery. From time to time the
recommendation of mesmeric treatment was made by various
individuals who had been impressed by mesmeric "experi-
ments," but a letter from her youngest sister, who was married

to a surgeon, describing a case of epilepsy apparently having
been cured by mesmerism, happened to coincide with the strong
urgings of her friend Basil Montague and his wife, so that she
began to think more seriously of the matter. Her sister Elizabeth's husband, Thomas Greenhow, who had acted as her physician throughout her illness, to her surprise acknowledged that
he had been favorably impressed by a lecture on mesmerism
given by Spencer Hall. He was agreeable to the notion of the
mesmeric experiment being conducted on his patient in the
hopes that it might provide "some release from the opiates to
which [she] was obliged to have constant recourse" (2:193).
Martineau kept a careful record of her mesmeric experiences
which she later published in 1844 as "Letters on Mesmerism"
in the *Athenaeum*. She experienced a progressive relief from
pain as a result of the hypnotic trances induced by Hall and
by a Mrs. Wynard as well as by her maid, Jane, who was able
to induce the same effect simply by imitating the gestures she
had seen Hall make. She found that her symptoms were steadily
receding, but her improved health was accompanied by annoyance on the part of her mother and her sister Rachel, since
they felt that a cure by such unconventional means effectively
slighted the professional reputation of Elizabeth's husband. There
was also a good deal of gossip about the cure, including public
discussion in the press. Martineau felt compelled to issue her
own version of the story and wrote to the editor of the *Athenaeum*
offering him six letters on mesmerism on the condition that
they were to be published unedited. Wary of the charge that
she was "rushing into print" to make a profit from her experiences, she stipulated that she wished the editor to donate any
payment that she would have received from the series to a charity
of his choice. To her horror, the *Athenaeum* published the letters
with appended editorial notes that attempted to discredit mesmerism in general and Martineau's experiences in particular.
The war of words about her illness and cure became an extremely bitter one when Greenhow published his account of
her case in a pamphlet entitled, *A Medical Report of the Case of
Miss H——— M———.*[8] Martineau had been asked by Greenhow
if she would permit him to publish an account of her case, and
she, believing that he intended to write a scientific account for
a medical journal, agreed. She was horrified, therefore, to find

a detailed gynecological account of her symptoms, "in a shilling pamphlet—not even written in Latin—but open to all the world!" (2:198). The main gist of this odd exercise in publicity was that Greenhow denied that he had ever regarded her condition as incurable and that he had always believed that her tumour was not malignant so that a spontaneous cure might easily occur. In fact, Greenhow had maintained throughout that her condition *was* incurable, and he evidently regarded her improvement in health as a threat to his professional reputation. Worse still, her mother and Rachel sided with Greenhow and felt that the infringement of Martineau's privacy was inconsequential compared with the threat to Greenhow's reputation as a physician.

The precise causes for the conflict and public controversy over Martineau's mesmeric cure are extremely difficult now to determine. Certainly, she was a public figure whose celebrity was only partly decreased by her retreat to a retired invalid life, and thus the crucial events of her life tended to become public property. The conflict between Martineau's desire to set the record straight and her family's urge to protect Greenhow's professional reputation was perhaps merely the vehicle for much of the covert resentment that some members of the family felt about her notoriety. Mesmerism was, it is true, a highly controversial subject. Although a number of famous figures, most notably Dickens, had experimented with mesmerism by mid-century, it still carried with it an aura of fairground charlatanism. By the latter part of the century, of course, Freud would be hypnotizing his patients in order to enable them to recall repressed experiences or fantasies, but despite the frequent use of mesmerism in a medical context, it never became established as a fully respectable medical practice. A modern reader is likely to be skeptical about whether Martineau's recovery was, as she claimed, due to the effects of mesmeric treatment, but may surmise rather that she was experiencing a spontaneous remission of symptoms which was aided by the psychological stimulus of the mesmeric "cure."

In many respects the extent of the attention attracted by her unexpected and unconventional recovery obscures the significance of much of her invalid period. There seems little doubt, contrary to the claims made in Webb's biography,[9] that she was indeed physiologically ill and that she experienced real physical distress. At the same time, it was a surprisingly productive period. In addition to *Life in the Sickroom,* she produced the four children's tales published as *The Playfellow* (1841), which remain among her most accomplished fiction. Away from the busy London literary scene, her life took a more meditative turn so that she was able to reflect much more directly on her serious doubts about the basic tenets of Unitarian Christianity.

The Atkinson Letters

It is difficult to evaluate the accuracy of Martineau's account of the gradual modifications of her religious belief in the *Autobiography.* Certainly her *Autobiography* was written in a somewhat defensive mood following the furor over the publication of the *Letters on the Laws and Nature of Man's Development* (1851). Her autobiographical account implies both that wrestling with religious and philosophical questions dominated much of Martineau's mental life and that her move away from Christian belief was more orderly, logical, and programmatic than it may, in fact, have been. Yet if we compare Martineau's autobiographical account of her self-questioning about Christian belief with that of other figures on the nineteenth-century literary and intellectual scene, she does not seem unusually preoccupied with religious doubt. While the convenient term "agnosticism" did not come into use until Thomas Huxley coined it in 1870, many Victorian intellectuals moved painfully from a devout Christianity to a philosophical position that fell short of assured atheism but nevertheless could no longer confidently assert a First Cause in the universe.

Martineau had, quite early in her life, given up the conventional Christian notion of prayer as supplication. She had also become disgusted at "the conception of life after death, as a matter of compensation for the ills of humanity, or a police and penal resource of 'the divine government'" (1:186). At the time when she wrote *Life in the Sickroom,* she still clung to the notion of an afterlife on the rather flimsy grounds that human "instinct" could not conceive of total extinction. Her Tynemouth meditations were, however, tending steadily in the direction of agnosticism:

I now began to obtain glimpses of the conclusion which at present seems to me so simple that it is a marvel why I waited for it so long;— that it is possible that we human beings with our mere human faculty, may not understand the scheme, or nature, of fact of the universe! I began to see that we, with our mere human faculty, are not in the least likely to understand it, any more than the minnow in the creek, as Carlyle has it, can comprehend the perturbations caused in his world of existence by the tides. (2:185)

In all probability, as for so many Victorian intellectuals, these reflections would have remained private and been only marginally reflected in her writing but for her acquaintance with Henry George Atkinson.

Atkinson seems an odd figure to the modern eye, but he was a familiar enough type in mid-nineteenth-century England. More or less a scientific and philosophical dilettante, Atkinson had dabbled a good deal in mesmerism and phrenology. Since scientific professionalism had not yet come into being, there was nothing immediately suspect, as there might be today, about the amateur nature of Atkinson's science. Some of Martineau's biographers express surprise at the extent to which Martineau seems to have been willing to accept the younger, intellectually inferior, Atkinson as her mentor and suggest that she may have been unconsciously in love with him. In some respects the relationship somewhat resembles that between George Eliot and John Chapman of the *Westminster Review* in which, although there was an overt sexual element, the older, more intellectually competent woman seems to have stood in uncritical awe of the rather spurious intellectual claims of a younger man. In the friendship between Martineau and Atkinson, however, sexual attraction does not seem to have played a significant role for either party. Martineau's behavior in this case can best be explained by the fact that she was, characteristically, an enthusiast, whether the subject was political economy, mesmerism, or the necessarian solution. She considered that mesmerism had saved her life, and Atkinson claimed to be able to place the significance of mesmerism within a grander philosophical scheme.

The *Letters* themselves are simply one of the many oddities

of nineteenth-century publishing. Martineau's part in the exchange is generally restricted to the role of enquirer, only occasionally chiding Atkinson for vagueness or self-contradiction.
Atkinson's letters, on the other hand, are long and rambling,
composed of a curious mish-mash of philosophical speculation
and confused religious rhetoric.

Surprisingly, the public response to the *Letters* was less preoccupied with their intellectual inadequacy than with their "plain,
avowed, ostentatious Atheism."[10] The reaction was a surprise
to Martineau herself who had been more concerned about how
the challenge to conventional Christianity in *Eastern Life* (1848)
would be received. Even the freethinking George Eliot thought
the letters "the boldest I have seen in the English language"
but, nonetheless, "studiously offensive."[11] Many of Martineau's
Lake District neighbors avoided her after the publication of
the *Letters.* The response was something of a surprise after the
quiet reception of *Eastern Life* three years earlier. Her insistence
that these slights were of no consequence to her was probably
overstated, but it seems credible enough that the response should
have reduced her respect for Christian belief: "I certainly had
no idea how little faith Christians have in their own faith till I
saw how ill their courage and temper can stand any attack upon
it" (2:354).

Much more painful was the vituperative attack launched on
the *Letters* by her brother James. His later claim that he only
undertook to write the review for the *Prospective Review* because
he was asked to do so and because another reviewer might
be harsher seems scanty enough. The review is a very lengthy
one, running to nearly forty pages, and it sets out systematically
to ridicule the *Letters,* focusing particularly on his sister's rather
than Atkinson's role in the publication. There seems little question that James's review was a deliberate attempt to inflict
wounding criticism on his sister and that the motive for this
was principally personal rather than theological. He seems to
have chosen to be deliberately obtuse about the likely effects
of his attack and even volunteered to review Martineau's translation of Comte in 1853. The other editors of the *Prospective Review*
seem to have had a clearer sense of his motives than James
himself was willing to admit, since his offer was rejected on
the grounds that "the editor was of the opinion that the work

would be criticized by Dr. Martineau in a thoroughly hostile spirit."[12] The review of the *Letters,* combined with James's deliberate obtuseness about the pain he had inflicted on his sister, brought communication to an end between them and Martineau neither saw nor wrote to her brother again.

The Complete Laker

Martineau made her first visit to the Lake District shortly before the onset of her long illness. After she became ill she felt that London was an unsuitable location for an invalid life and gravitated toward the north of England, not however at this time the Lake District, but the quiet seaside town of Tynemouth. Once her recovery was complete, she rejected the idea of returning to live in London. She was reluctant to fall into a "hackney coach and company life" and felt the need for her own domestic establishment. Although she was not explicit about the point, as an established rather than an aspiring author she no longer needed to court literary connections in London but could be confident that her work would be sought out, even though she lived at a distance from the main cultural centre. The Lake District was, at this period, either the permanent home or the frequent resort of many prominent literary figures. Wordsworth, the region's best known native son, lived at Rydall Mount, with Matthew Arnold not very far away at Fox How. During the summer, visitors from literary London flocked to the area. The Lake District attracted Martineau for other reasons. It seemed the ideal place in which to establish "a house of my own among poor improvable neighbours with young servants whom I might train and attach to myself; with pure air, a garden, leisure, solitude at command, and freedom to work in peace and quietness" (2:225).

Undoubtedly, this final period of her life was the most contented. Her purchase of a plot of land, the building of her house at Ambleside, and her practical schemes for managing a small farming operation on her few acres are all lovingly and absorbedly recounted both in the *Autobiography* and in *Health, Husbandry and Handicraft* (1861). Even in her earliest writings she had shown an intense interest in and admiration for thrifty and practical domestic and agricultural management. At Ambleside, she had, for the first time, an opportunity to put her theories into practice, and she evidently relished the experience.

She resumed prolific literary production, translating Comte, traveling in Egypt, and writing *Eastern Life,* and in 1852 began writing regular leader columns for the *Daily News.* This was accompanied by a vigorous physical life. She generally rose very early in the morning, taking a long walk before breakfast and beginning the day's writing. Her neighbor, Wordsworth, who associated his sister Dorothy's habit of walking long distances with the deterioration in her health and her eventual madness, viewed these activities with serious alarm. On one occasion she met Wordsworth while she was out walking with Atkinson: " 'There, there!' said Wordsworth, laying his hand on my companion's arm. 'Take care! take care! Don't let *her* carry you about. She is killing off half the gentlemen in the county!' " (2:238).

She also busied herself with supervising the running of her small farm, becoming something of an enthusiast on "cow-keeping" and even writing two essays on the subject. Her efforts at "improving" her neighbors were generally practical rather than, in the favorite fashion of the day, moral and spiritual. She founded a small-scale building society to provide sound cottage housing for workers at reasonable prices and gave lectures during the winter on such subjects as "Sanitary Principles and Practices" and "The History of North America."

When the Ambleside house was finished, Martineau had a small sundial placed in the garden. The usual religious mottoes commonly used on sundials were inappropriate for a skeptic so she devised her own, "Come Light! Visit me!" It seems a suitable coda for this phase of her life, epitomizing the mood and quality of the years between her recovery from her illness and the writing of the *Autobiography.*

Yielding Her Place in the Universe

By 1854, Martineau sensed that she was, once more, seriously ill. The symptoms were very different from those of sixteen years earlier. She was experiencing spells of dizziness and she suspected heart trouble. After consulting two London physicians, she was certain that her heart was seriously affected and that she could not expect to live long. The source of her symptoms seems to have been an enlargement of the tumour that had been the origin of her first illness at Tynemouth but which was now causing breathlessness and interference with the normal operation of the heart. She insisted, however, that this illness was very different from "the Tynemouth disease." As Pichanick suggests, this insistence probably sprang from a reluctance to let the critics of her mesmeric cure get the better of her, but it was also probably true that because of the change in the tumour's position and its enlargement, the symptoms she now experienced were very different from those she remembered at Tynemouth.

Believing that she was dying, she felt that her first task must be to write her autobiography. She had always intended to do so, especially since her life "became evidently a somewhat re-markable one" (1:1). She had made a start as early as 1831 and again during the Tynemouth period, but both attempts had done little more than record some of her childhood experiences. Now, especially since she had earlier asked all her correspon-dents to destroy her letters, she felt it her clear duty to provide her own record. Written in this frame of mind, despite the criticisms it received when first published, Harriet Martineau's *Autobiography* remains one of the great, if rarely read, autobiog-raphies of an age that was beginning to produce extraordinary biographical and autobiographical writing.

Part of the vividness and coherence of Martineau's *Autobiogra-phy* springs from Martineau's attitude toward what she believed to be her own imminent death. She emphasized that her belief that there was no life after death did not increase her fear of death. Rather, the necessarian view had helped her to realize "how the universe will go on just the same whether one dies at fifty or seventy" (2:208). Such an attitude, she stressed, en-hanced rather than dimmed her "relish of life," yet she felt "no reluctance whatever to pass into nothingness, leaving my place in the universe to be filled by another" (2:207).

In fact, although she never again enjoyed the good health of the ten years immediately following her recovery from her Tynemouth invalidism, the deterioration of her health was very slow, enabling her to write fairly prolifically during the first ten of the twenty-two years that remained to her. She revised

editions of her earlier works and wrote regular editorials for
the *Daily News* four or five times each week. She kept up a
busy correspondence including a particularly active one with
Florence Nightingale, whose work sometimes prompted subjects
for her columns in the *News.* On one notable occasion, Nightingale was worried that Sir George Cornewall Lewis would be
selected as minister for war and sent Martineau an urgent tele-
gram, "Agitate, Agitate for Lord de Gray in place of Sir G.
Cornewall Lewis."[13] Martineau immediately wrote a strong
leader for the *Daily News* which was probably influential in
ensuring that Lord de Gray became minister.

Later political collaboration with Nightingale was to prove
even more demanding. Efforts were being made to create a
system of registration for the prostitutes who followed the army.
Florence Nightingale had collected copious statistics to show
that the "continental system" of licensed brothels did not reduce
the incidence of venereal disease. The proposed Contagious
Diseases Acts permitted the forcible medical inspection for venereal disease of any woman in military towns, such as Aldershot,
on the suspicion that she was a prostitute. The soldiers themselves were not required to be examined. Florence Nightingale,
Josephine Butler, and Harriet Martineau published *An Appeal
to the Women of England,* denouncing the Contagious Diseases
Acts and signed by a number of influential women. Their appeal
pointed out that the acts essentially designated *all* women as
prostitutes and they affirmed, "it is unjust to punish the sex
who are the victims of a vice and leave unpunished the sex
who are the main cause" (3:431–32). Largely as a result of
their continued efforts, the two Contagious Diseases Acts of
1866 and 1869 were repealed in 1871.

The greatest sadness of this final period of Martineau's life
was, undoubtedly, the death from typhoid of her niece Maria
who had long been her valued companion in the Ambleside
house. Her death, Martineau confided to a correspondent, was
"a shake not to be got over."[14] Her sister Jane took Maria's
place as Martineau's companion at the Knoll but never quite
replaced Maria in Martineau's affections.

Her final years were shadowed, not only by personal bereave-
ments and illness, but also by difficult financial circumstances.
Some of her investments no longer paid a dividend and she

and Jane were forced to establish a more rigorous domestic economy. It was suggested by one of the editors of the *Daily News* that her biographical essays on her various contemporaries for that paper could easily be turned into a book, which resulted in the publication of *Biographical Sketches,* a work that provides us with some uniquely telling portraits of a wide range of significant figures of the period.

The biographical sketches eventually published in book form had all been originally written with the intention of serving as obituaries when their subjects died. Not one to leave such a thing to chance, Martineau provided a similar obituary for herself. Although it was written during the same period as the *Autobiography* many years before her death, it still serves as an amazingly clear-headed and objective account of her place as a writer and a popular figure.

Harriet Martineau finally concluded the life in which, in her own words, she "worked hard and usefully, won friends, reputation and independence, saw the world abundantly, abroad and at home" (1:142), at the Knoll, Ambleside on 27 June, 1876. Despite the retirement in which she had lived her final years, there is no question that the periodicals of the day and the correspondence of her contemporaries noted her death with an evident sense that a figure of considerable stature had vanished from the Victorian literary and political scene.

Chapter Two

"A Trumpet of Remarkable Fidelity": Martineau's Travel Writings

Travels in America

During the first half of the nineteenth century it was a common phenomenon for English writers and journalists to travel to America and, on their return, to translate their adventures and observations into profit in the form of a popular book on their experiences. This pattern of reportage became both widely read and highly controversial on either side of the Atlantic. Captain Basil Hall established himself early as "the arch traitor to American hospitality"[1] with his fault-finding *Travels in North America in the years 1827 and 1828.* Not surprisingly, Americans were resentful of the criticisms of their public, social, and domestic life that many English writers during the period seemed ready to mete out in such a patronizing manner. Although when Harriet Martineau set out from Liverpool in 1834, the prospect of a British writer passing judgment on American mores and manners was not yet the minefield it was to become by mid-century, Martineau was still acutely conscious that her visit might give rise to unfavorable comment. From the beginning, she insisted that her trip was not "a book making expedition" (2:2), and indeed she refused several financially attractive offers from would-be publishers. There seems to be no reason to doubt this initial resolve. It is readily apparent that she felt drained by the breakneck speed with which she wrote many of the *Illustrations of Political Economy.* Yet, characteristically, she thrusts the need for a rest from writing aside in favor of a more morally demanding objective: "My first desire was for rest. My next was to break through any selfish 'particularity' that might be growing on me with years, and any love of ease and indulgence that might have arisen out of success, flattery, or the devoted kindness of my friends. I believed that it would be good for me to 'rough it' for a while, before I grew too old and fixed in my habits for such an experiment." It is evident, however, that she began her journey in a state of mental enervation. She had committed herself to write a short book under the title *How to Observe Morals and Manners* (1838) for Charles Knight. She completed her obligation during the course of the voyage, but it is evident from the flat tone of the work itself and from her references to it in her *Autobiography* that she fulfilled this minor chore with scanty enthusiasm. The work was intended to be the first of a series of volumes each of which was to focus on a different aspect of "how to observe." Written in an atypically verbose style, it is not much more than a lengthy essay that anticipates many of the observations she would make about American institutions and social mores.

Society in America and *Retrospect of Western Travel*

Martineau set out to observe American society and to record her observations in a systematic rather than an impressionistic way. This approach is reflected in the structure of *Society in America*. Divided into three sections, the first deals with political and legislative institutions, the second with economics, and the third with social mores and cultural life. She scrutinizes all these aspects of American life both in relation to her views on political economy and according to the egalitarian principles on which the country had been established. She focuses closely on the differences between British and American agricultural practices, examining the effects of slave labor on the rural economy, and devotes considerable attention to the position of women in American society. The descriptions she offers of social institutions tend to be concrete rather than abstract through her extensive use of personal anecdotes.

Retrospect of Western Travel, published in the following year, was less ambitious in outline and did not attempt to provide a definitive portrait of American society, but rather a personal account of her journey. Although Martineau's intense interest in social institutions is still evident it becomes the background for a personal travel narrative in which the traveler's moods and impressions dominate. The second book is organized around the sequence of places visited rather than the sociological model used for *Society in America.*

One of the reasons Martineau was cautious about committing herself to a travel book on America was that such a commitment would readily have been interpreted as an intent to use the books as a vehicle for her abolitionist views. Her antislavery tale, *Demerara* (1832), in the political economy series, had already made her a notorious figure in the Southern states. It is evident from both *Society in America* and *Retrospect of Western Travel* that Martineau was not susceptible to intimidation in relation to her antislavery views, but, at the same time, she was reluctant to make public statements on the subject since she insisted that the purpose of her visit was to learn and not to teach.

Unlike many English travel writers, Martineau had, from the outset, a buoyantly optimistic view of the New World. The physical vastness of the land, its potential wealth, the idealism of its Constitution, all inspired her with high hopes for the future of the country. She declared that she saw little or no poverty and, with her usual trenchant sense of combining phrase and example, remarks, "Every factory child carries its umbrella and pig-drivers wear spectacles."[2] Always, she is hopeful about America's future in view of "the vast materials of human happiness which are placed at the disposal of the real administrators of this country."[3] She regards politicians as frequently too limited in their views of the nation's possibilities as, for example, when the Democratic party of the day argued that the states were essentially intended to be agricultural, she counters, "It seems to me that they are intended to be everything" (*S,* 2:31). The possibility of a genuinely revolutionary society is always in her mind and she argues that in America property itself will eventually become obsolete (*S,* 2:56).

Despite her distress at the paradox of slavery being tolerated within the Constitution, she is enthusiastic about the Constitution itself as one based on "philosophy" and inductive reasoning rather than on ancient precedents derived from a feudal society. Nevertheless, she is aware that self-government makes for a complexity in political life that is unknown under "a pure despotism" (*S*, 1:110) and gives this as her justification for the extensive attention paid to public and political life in *Society in America.*

Martineau as Observer and Traveler

No doubt aware that the accuracy of her observation might be called into question because of her deafness, Martineau is quick to provide an assessment of how far her handicap limited her observation. She admits that she is disadvantaged by being unable to overhear "the casual conversation of all kinds of people in the streets, stages, hotels, etc.," and that such inadvertent eavesdropping is often far more informative to the traveler "than the most elaborate accounts of things offered to him with an express design" (*S*, 1:xviii). Nevertheless, she is undaunted in presenting her information as accurate because she possesses "a trumpet of remarkable fidelity; an instrument, moreover, which seems to exert some winning power, by which I gain more in tête-à-têtes than is given to people who hear general conversation" (*S*, 1:xvii–xviii).

If her deafness limited the scope of her observations, then she compensated through the extent of her travels which were unusually wide-ranging for an English visitor of the time. In all, she traveled over ten thousand miles by road and inland waterways, extending her travels further west than was common during the 1830s. Equally unusual, before steamboat travel had been initiated on the Great Lakes, she crossed Lake Erie by boat from Chicago to Milwaukee. While other English travelers were often content to restrict their observations on "America" to the major cities of the Eastern seaboard, Martineau's journey takes her as far south as New Orleans, then up the Mississippi by riverboat. She traveled through Tennessee, Kentucky, and into Ohio before ending her journey with a series of trips throughout New England. Her visits to prisons and other institutions, to Niagara Falls, and to hear Daniel Webster speak in court were conventional enough items on the early nineteenth-century traveler's itinerary, yet her observations on all these are characterized by a perspicacity that often makes the accounts of other travelers seem somewhat flaccid by comparison.

As a traveling companion, Martineau is both engaging and exhausting. On the ocean voyage from Liverpool to New York, when the ship runs into a hurricane and the ladies' cabin is intolerable from "the crashing of glass, the complaining voices of the sick ladies, the creaking and straining of the ship; and above all, the want of air, while the winds were roaring overhead," she conquers her sickness to go on deck and is so impressed with the grandeur of the storm that she stumbles back to the cabin "to implore the other ladies to come and be refreshed" (*R,* 1:28). They pay no attention but she persuades the captain to allow her to lash herself to the binnacle post from which position she not only observes the storm but also the varied effects of terror on the other passengers.

Continually, throughout her travels, her curiosity is able to overcome either fear or discomfort. In Kentucky, she watches a "bee-tree" being felled and goes to see the swarm at close quarters, returning to her companions "stung, but having seen what I wanted" (*S,* 1:275). Traveling on the Hudson, she rises between three and five in the morning to watch the sunrise. When the stage becomes stuck in yet another pothole she prefers to walk on alone, "sure of not missing my road in a region where there was no other" rather than wait for an hour or more while the sunken wheel is being freed (*S,* 1:175). As always, she is an indefatigable walker. During her stay in New England she sets off for a five-mile walk to Lenox while her friends prefer to travel in a wagon. Her host's son comments on her pace, "I would not walk off at that rate, if they gave me Lenox when I got there" (*S,* 1:266).

She is often amazed at the bored or blasé attitude of other travelers. In Massachusetts she persuades her fellow travelers to rise at four to see the sunrise, explaining when asked that she wishes to see "its effect . . . on the landscape." To her astonishment, she met with the reply, "Upon the landscape! Oh but we saw that yesterday" (*R,* 1:62–63). Similarly, when traveling up the Mississippi, she finds it extraordinary that most of the female passengers remain in the ladies' cabin and "never look out of the boat unless their attention [is] particularly called" (*R,* 2:11). She is equally impatient with the false effusiveness that was often affected by female travelers of the time. One woman questions her at length about what emotions she experiences at Niagara Falls and asks gushingly, "Did you not long to throw yourself down and mingle with your mother Earth."

"No," Martineau laconically replies (*S*, 3:81). She is also critical of the bad manners of other English travelers whom she meets, especially when they are faultfinding and peevish. At Niagara Falls she encounters a traveler who is, "so incessantly pettish, so resolutely miserable, as to bespeak the compassion of all the guests for the ladies in his family" (*R*, 1:99). When he finds the falls at Niagara less impressive than the falls of the British River Clyde, she concludes, "Such are the persons by whom foreigners suppose themselves made acquainted with the English character. Such is the way in which not a few English study to mortify the inhabitants, and then come home and complain of American conceit" (*R*, 1:99).

Her own attention is so actively engaged in her travels that she rarely complains about any of the discomforts of the journey. Even the terrible condition of the roads, a major target for other English visitors who had been mercilessly jolted or overturned during their travels, gives her no cause for complaint. When she and her fellow travelers are served with a meat of dubious origin she recalls, "When the dinner was on the table, no one of us could tell what it consisted of. The dish from which I ate was, according to some, mutton; to others, pork: my own idea is that it was dog" (*S*, 1:259).

It is obvious that her appetite is not especially blunted by the speculation. During the latter part of her journey, it is evident that Martineau exerts some of her energies in organizing an efficient itinerary for herself and her fellow travelers and that her earnestness in accomplishing this turned her into a somewhat comic figure in the eyes of her companions: "There was also a joke against me. I was now a practised traveler; and having found how the pleasures of traveling are economized by business-like habits of arrangement, I was the prompter of our somewhat inexperienced party about ordering dinner, packing at convenient times, and so contriving as to have our thoughts at perfect liberty for pleasure while we were out of doors, instead of having to run or send to our lodgings about business which might have been settled while we were there" (*R*, 1:106–7). Yet it is plain that her approach to travel is never that of the petty tourist with a mental checklist of "sights." Rather, she is capable of being deeply moved by the unexpected; clinging to a pine stem at Hawk's Nest overlooking the Kanawha

river on the Allegheny Plateau she feels that her future can
hold few more impressive sights: "With each arm clasping a
pine-stem, I looked over, and saw more, I cannot but think,
than the world has in reserve to show me" (*S*, 1:243).

An Englishwoman's View of America

Like other English travelers of the period, Martineau is clearly
impressed both with the sheer vastness of the country and with
the configuration of the landscape. Frequently the physical grandeur of the landscape brings to her mind a sense of geological
time and the insignificant space occupied by the individual human experience in such a vast canvas. Sitting outside the Mam-
moth Cave in Kentucky, she sees a rich growth of kalmias and,
amid her own delight at their beauty, comments, "How apt
are we to look upon all things as made for us! How many
seasons has this kalmia bloomed?" (*S*, 1:235). Yet it is not
merely her own ego which she finds insignificant in the face
of the vastness of the continent. On being told that Hawk's
Nest was "discovered" by Chief Justice Marshall as a young
man surveying the mountains, she comments succinctly, "Nature's thrones are not left to be first mounted by men who
can be made Chief Justices. We know not what races of wild
monarchs may have had them first"(*S*, 1:244).

Inevitably, she finds herself comparing American life and manners with the English, and, in general, these comparisons favor
the New World over the Old. The issue of slavery aside, she
is profoundly impressed by American egalitarianism. Many English travelers were critical of the "superficial" nature of education in American schools and colleges, but Martineau is more
interested in the fact that a basic education is much more widely
available than in England: "Their . . . schools . . . are exciting
and feeding thousands of minds, which in England would never
get beyond the loom or the ploughtail. If very few are very
learned in the villages of Massachussets, still fewer are very
ignorant . . ." (*R*, 2:91). Many travel writers, especially Mrs.
Trollope in her *Domestic Manners of the Americans* (1832), denounced the vulgarity of American manners, but Martineau,
although she, like other travelers, is repulsed by the extensive
use of tobacco and the concomitant spitting, is emphatic that

encountering bad manners is a rarity. She speaks highly of American hospitality and declares that Americans are "the most good-tempered people in the world" (*S*, 2:54). Her only real annoyance about the matter is caused by the boorish behavior of land-speculators on the boat crossing from Chicago to Milwaukee. Elsewhere the egalitarian quality of social life and manners causes her to comment on the "aristocratic insolence" that characterizes manners in England and to remark that "Nothing in American civilisation struck me so forcibly and so pleasurably as the invariable respect paid to man as man. Nothing since my return to England has given me so much pain as the contrast there" (*S*, 3:27). She is delighted, too, at the physical freedom and skill of American children compared with their English peers, and she finds their readiness to converse with adult strangers a pleasing contrast to the artificially constrained social manners of English children. The only group she seems to find inferior to its English counterpart is the American criminal. She recounts the story of the Philadelphia burglar who broke into a house and, after giving up the search for something worth stealing, is about to leave when he discovers that it has begun to rain. He steals an umbrella and this leads to his arrest. "What English burglar would have thought of minding the rain?" (*S*, 2:247), Martineau scornfully asks.

American Cultural Life

Although she is impressed with a Mozart concert in Cincinnati and recommends the paintings of James Henry Beard, Martineau's interest in the arts in America is focused almost entirely upon literature. Like other English writers, she bemoans the lack of copyright laws, which permitted American publishers to republish the works of English or other foreign authors without payment. But, unlike Dickens, who was to make himself unpopular with American audiences through his speeches on the subject, her interest in the issue ranges well beyond its effect on her own earnings as a writer. She examines the argument made by some that the bad copyright laws were responsible for what we would now call "cultural imperialism" whereby the preponderance of the artistic, literary, and intellectual productions of a foreign country overwhelm indigenous arts. Characteristically, she argues that the genuinely outstanding American writer can still win through "a host of bookselling harpies, and a chaos of lawlessness . . . even if it had been necessary to give his dinner for paper, and sell his bed to pay the printer . . ." (*S*, 3:218).

Her assessment of contemporary American writers is interestingly at variance with more recent evaluations. She dismisses Cooper's novels and prefers the stories of Catherine Sedgewick to those of Washington Irving: "She sympathizes where he good-naturedly observes; she cheerily loves where he gently quizzes" (*S*, 3:213). She admires Bryant the poet and Bancroft the historian, is vastly impressed by Emerson as an individual as well as a writer, and speaks highly of the literary merits of the *Knicker-bocker* magazine. She observes that the British author most admired by Americans is Hannah More and remarks, "She is much better known in the country than Shakespeare" (*S*, 3:219). She hears much admiration of Maria Edgeworth's work, but suspects that Bulwer Lytton's novels are more widely read. Oddly, she concludes that "Wordsworth lies at the heart of the people" (*S*, 3:219), yet she admits that he has rarely been mentioned to her by Americans. Evidently she regards Wordsworth's themes and preoccupations as especially appropriate for Americans and is able to transform this sense of appropriateness into the belief that his works were, in fact, widely read.

American Public Life

As an admirer of American political institutions themselves, Martineau tended to be critical of any inconsistencies in their operation. Slavery was, of course, the prime example of a gross paradox between political ideals and actual practice, but she is also critical of some lesser inconsistencies such as the practice of electing judges for life, a procedure she regarded as entirely inappropriate in a democratic republic. She finds much of the rhetoric of political speeches considerably too florid for her taste and is particularly offended by the self-congratulatory and flattering tone of the speech she hears an ex-senator deliver on Forefather's Day in Plymouth.

Throughout her life Martineau had an acute interest in public and political life, although her political status as a woman prevented her from participating directly except as a journalist. Though she does not mention her own unenfranchised status in this particular context, it is surely part of the stimulus for the intense concern with which she views political apathy. When a clergyman complacently indicates his lack of interest in voting, she remarks, "This gentleman had probably never heard of the old lady who said that she did not care what revolutions happened, as long as she had her roast chicken, and her little game at cards. But that old lady did not live in a republic, or perhaps even she might have perceived that there would have been no security for roast chickens and cards, if all were to neglect political action but those who want political power and profit" (*S*, 1:155–56). Elsewhere, she places political apathy and ignorance of major events in a wider historical perspective and suggests that at all phases of history the majority of the people know or care very little about the great events of their time: "I suppose while Luther was toiling and thundering, German ladies and gentlemen were supping and dancing as usual; and while the Lollards were burning, perhaps little was known or cared about it in warehouses and upon farms. So it was in America" (*R*, 2:159). She is acutely aware of the importance of the role played by newspapers in a democratic society and is highly critical of the self-censorship practiced by American papers on the slavery issue. Her account suggests that the majority of newspapers are openly corrupt in suppression of facts and promulgating falsehoods about certain political candidates, while the few responsibly conducted papers languish for the lack of the "encouragement" of a large audience. She is outraged by the cowardice of Southern newspapers whose editors privately condemned but publicly acceded to such crimes as the burning alive of a man in St. Louis and describes such newspapers as worthy of comparison with an "unfaithful mastiff, if such a creature there be" (*S*, 1:152).

The Condition of Women

Although she admits that the legal situation of married women in the United States was better than in England, she compares the legal status of women in America as technically equivalent to that of slaves in that all the political choices that affected their lives were made for them by others. That some women acquiesce to such a status and even claim that they prefer it proves only, she argues, "the degradation of the injured party. It inspires the same emotions of pity as the supplication of the freed slave who kneels to his master to restore him to slavery, that he may have his animal wants supplied, without being troubled with human rights and duties" (S, 1:204). She is acerbic about the social "chivalry" extended to women as a fraudulent deception and attacks the fallacy that the role of men is to "protect" women, pointing out that male "protection" is useless against the real trials that any individual woman must face: "He can neither secure any woman from pain and grief, nor rescue her from the strife of emotions, nor prevent the film of life from cracking under her feet with every step she treads, nor hide from her the abyss which is beneath, nor save her from sinking into it at last alone" (S, 3:116). This spurious "protection" serves only, she argues, to weaken each individual woman's strength and resolve. She observes that this artificial protectiveness toward women extends even to the way in which women in America are constantly referred to as "ladies," citing as the most absurd example of this usage the religious lecturer "discoursing on the characteristics of women, [who] is said to have expressed himself thus: 'Who were last at the cross? Ladies. Who were first at the sepulchre? Ladies'" (S, 3:84). She is disparaging about the way in which well-off women collude with the notion of being in need of protection and is especially exasperated with the affectations of such women when they are traveling: "While on a journey, women who appear well enough in their homes, present all the characteristics of spoiled children. Screaming and trembling at the apprehension of danger are not uncommon: but there is something far worse in the cool selfishness with which they accept the best of everything, at any sacrifice to others, and usually, in the south and west, without a word or look of acknowledgement" (S, 3:90). She is also disturbed at the frivolous and disruptive behavior of the legislators' wives and daughters in the ladies' gallery at a Senate debate. She sees the silly and affected behavior of such women as the inevitable end product of the attitude that promotes women's indolence as a positive virtue.

She is particularly concerned about the difficulties of working women in a country where the idea of women not working is presented as so desirable. She enumerates some of the employment possibilities open to poor women in factories and in mills, but she is less sanguine about the traditional resort of single middle-class women, employment as a governess: "Let philanthropists inquire into the proportion of governesses among the inmates of lunatic asylums. The answer to this question will be found to involve a world of rebuke and instruction" (*S,* 3:149). She is told by one man who expressed an interest in the subject that the trend in American society was to make women more rather than less dependent, and that individual women could only break through "conventional restraints" as a result of "genius or calamity." "The first," he concludes, "is too rare a circumstance to afford any basis for speculation: and may Heaven avert the last!" Martineau, perhaps with some sense of herself as one who had been freed from conventional restraints by means of the "calamity" of her family's loss of fortune, exclaims, "O, may Heaven hasten it! . . . There are, I believe, some who would scarcely tremble to see their houses in flames, to hear the coming tornado, to feel the threatening earthquake, if these be indeed messengers who must open their prison doors, and give their heaven-born spirits the range of the universe . . ." (*S,* 2:340).

Slavery

Perhaps aware that her views on slavery would be especially subject to scrutiny when her book was published, Martineau is careful throughout to couch her argument in cool, rational terms. She never bases her argument explicitly on the grounds of racial equality, declaring that it "bears no relation to the question," but instead argues that slavery is an anomaly in relation to the Constitution and that "an anomaly among a self-governing people" will soon disappear. She states confidently, "Its doom is therefore sealed; and its duration is now merely a question of time" (*S,* 1:108).

It is evident, however, that despite the deliberately dispassionate tone of her formal argument against slavery, she was deeply moved by the condition of slaves. She was profoundly uncomfortable when accepting hospitality compelled her to receive

the services of slaves, and the frequency of the experience in
no way served to inure her to her distress: "No familiarity
with them, no mirth and contentment on their part, ever soothed
the miserable restlessness caused by the presence of a deeply-
injured fellow-being" (*R,* 1:141). In her account of her visit
to a slave market ("a place which the traveler ought not to
avoid to spare his feelings") she is plainly profoundly distressed,
not only at the misery of the slaves, but at the "jocose zeal"
with which the auction is conducted. When a woman complacently comments to her while a mother and her child are being
sold that the subservience of one race to another is natural
and that she would willingly exchange places with the woman
on the block if the social situation were reversed, Martineau
grimly reflects, "Who could help saying within himself, 'Would
you were! so that that mother were released!' " (*R,* 1:235).

Despite the intensity of her feelings on the subject, she persists
in using logic rather than emotion as the most potent weapon
in discussion. She is frequently told by Southerners that slaves
prefer slavery to freedom, citing in support some instances of
freed slaves who have returned to their former masters. She
argues that the inability of some to tolerate freedom only speaks
more eloquently of the degrading effect of slavery on the individual. On another occasion she is able to turn her opponents'
argument that slaves really prefer slavery directly to her own
advantage. She is told of a slave who prevented a church from
being burned down and who was rewarded by being given
his liberty:

"A reward!" said I. "What! when the slaves are convinced that
their true happiness lies in slavery?"
The conversation had come to an awkward pass. A lady advanced
to the rescue, saying that some few, too many, were haunted by a
pernicious fancy, put into their heads by others, about liberty; a mere
fancy, which, however, makes them like the idea of freedom.
"So the benefactor of the city was rewarded by being indulged,
to his own hurt, in a pernicious fancy?"
"Why . . . yes." (*R,* 1:240)

Martineau's argument against slavery in *Demerara* was, because of its context in the political economy series, an economic

one. The broader scope of the travel books and her direct experience of slavery in action enable her to comment on the impact
of slavery on other aspects of society. She observes that intense
hatred exists between the slave owner and the slave, not, as
one might expect, generated from the slave toward the owner,
but rather on the part of the slave owner toward the slave.
She points out that the "endearing relation" between master
and slave of which Southerners often spoke only exists while
the slave is totally docile: "But, from the moment he exhibits
the attributes of a rational being—from the moment his intellect
seems likely to come into the most distant competition with
that of whites, the most deadly hatred springs up;—not in the
black, but in his oppressors" (*S,* 2:152–53). In some respects
she is more distressed by the opaque unconscious prejudice
displayed by those who have "liberal" views than by the irre-
deemably bigoted. She hears a preacher declare in a sermon
that "God cares for all,—for the meanest as well as the mightiest.
'He cares for that coloured person,' said he, pointing to the
gallery where the people of colour sit,—'he cares for that coloured person as well as for the whitest and best of you whites.' "
Martineau is stunned at what she describes as "the most wanton
insult I had ever seen offered to a human being" (*S,* 2:335)
and is tempted to walk out of the church, but is even more
astonished that her companions are bewildered that she could
find anything objectionable in the sermon.

She sees the effects of slavery as debilitating to the whole
social fabric of the South and is contemptuous about the idle
vapid life led by Southern slave owners. Most of all, she is
disturbed about the values inevitably imbibed by children in
such a society: "When children at school call everything that
pleases them 'gentlemanly,' and pity all (but slaves) who have
to work, and talk of marrying early for an establishment, it is
all over with them" (*S,* 2:308). Many of the values learned
by the children are learned unconsciously, from example, she
suggests, even though specific moral teaching runs counter to
their everyday experience.

Martineau was able to write more openly of the sexual dimension of slavery than would have been possible for a writer later
in the century, and she shows her concern, not only for the
slave women prostituted to white men, but of the poisonous

effect of men's duplicity on their marriages: "Every white lady believes that her husband has been an exception to the rule of seduction. What security for domestic purity and peace there can be where every man has had two connections, one of which must be concealed; and two families, whose existence must not be known to each other; where the conjugal relation begins in treachery, and must be carried on with a heavy secret in the husband's breast, no words are needed to explain" (*S*, 2:327).

Considering her well-known and strongly held views on slavery, it is somewhat surprising that Martineau was at first reluctant to associate with prominent American abolitionists. During the early part of her visit she seems to have placed some credence in the smears against the activities of abolitionists that were disseminated by the pro-slavery faction. Her views swiftly changed when she met some of the abolitionists in person and became aware of the extent to which the North colluded with slavery both by returning escaped slaves to their owners and by suppressing the abolitionist movement. Her private convictions became public when she received an invitation to an antislavery meeting in Boston. Her first concern was for the reputation and safety of her host who has already been pilloried merely for reading a notice of an antislavery meeting from the pulpit. Eventually she makes up her mind to attend and her hosts' response is an index of the gravity of her decision: "Between joke and earnest, they told us we should be mobbed; and the same thing was repeated by many who were not in joke at all" (*R*, 2:162). At the meeting she is handed a note requesting her to speak in support of abolitionist aims, and while she knows that, "Having thus declared myself on the safe side of the Atlantic I was bound to act on the unsafe side, if called upon" (*R*, 2:163), she is nonetheless perturbed since she fears that her openly partisan stance will limit her capacity as an observer and that she will be seen as "a missionary or a spy" (*R*, 2:164). In reflecting on the results of her public statement she concurs that "distant observers" might well conclude from the "hubbub" that "the whole nation had risen against me" (*R*, 2:164). However, she insists that this reaction was the work of a very small group and that her role as observer was unhampered.

When Martineau set sail from New York, her travels and the friendships she had formed had made such an impression on her that she was by no means certain that she would not soon return to "live and die in America." Her domestic duties in caring for her mother and her own long illness intervened, and thus Martineau's place in American letters remained that of a sympathetic and perspicacious observer.

The two American travel books served to consolidate the reputation Martineau had established through her *Illustrations of Political Economy*. Both *Society in America* and *Retrospect of Western Travel* were well received by reviewers and readers on both sides of the Atlantic, although her English audience tended to find the second book more approachable than the ambitious *Society in America*. Conservative readers in both countries, however, tended to react against the apparently radical social views implied in her account of American society.

Eastern Life, Present and Past

Like so many important events in Harriet Martineau's life, the journey that led to what is perhaps her best travel book came about partly by chance. Having, as a personal favor, let her Ambleside house to a honeymoon couple, she set off to Liverpool to visit her youngest sister, "Little dreaming how long it would be before I came back again" (2:269). During her stay in Liverpool, she renewed her acquaintance with Richard Yates and his wife who were planning an extensive Eastern tour. Yates persuaded Martineau to allow him to pay her travel expenses so that she could accompany them. They were to be joined by J. C. Ewart, the member of Parliament for Liverpool, who later proved to be a most valuable asset to their company. Given Martineau's intense independence in matters of personal finances, it is somewhat surprising that she agreed with such alacrity to allow Yates to finance her journey, but evidently the open and unreserved nature of Yates's offer combined with her own sense of the uniqueness of the opportunity to persuade her that this was not the time to be stubbornly independent.

Unquestionably, there were many inducements to recommend such a journey. Many years earlier, in her book *Traditions of Palestine* (1830), she had tried to show something of the histori-

cal context of the Bible. The book's broad approach and direct
style led to its being reprinted a number of times, yet its sub-
stance is fairly slight. Martineau took the Unitarian line of showing how Christian doctrines had arisen from specific cultural
and historical origins, and she implied that those doctrines
should therefore be flexible to accommodate current conditions.
Despite this fairly liberal approach to religious belief, *Traditions
of Palestine* follows the essential form and tone of the conventional devotional essay of the time.

Martineau's questioning of the foundations of Christian belief
had only been hinted at in *Traditions of Palestine,* but it was to
become more and more conscious during the 1830s, so that
by the time she undertook her Eastern tour she could call herself
a Christian, "if at all, only in the free-thinking sense" (1:158).
Unlike other nineteenth-century intellectuals, Martineau's arrival at the philosophical position which we would now describe
as "agnostic" took place not as a result of a dark night of the
soul of the kind experienced by J. S. Mill and others, but by
means of a series of modifications of conventional Christian belief. She continued all her life to believe that it was quite possible
that the universe had had a first cause, but maintained that its
attributes were unknowable. Although she eventually ceased
to believe in the possibility of life after death, at the time of
her Eastern journey she still believed that immortality might
exist, not as a scriptural promise, but simply as a natural phenomenon. The prospect of the Eastern tour offered her the opportunity of putting her religious views in context, providing a
historical and geographical perspective on the study of the Bible,
which was impossible in Ambleside or London.

In contrast to her American travel books, in *Eastern Life* Martineau seems to have consciously intended to cast a benign rather
than a critical eye on Eastern society. The epigraph to the book,
from Francis Bacon's *Advancement of Learning,* sets the tone:
"Joyful to receive the impression thereof, as the eye joyeth to
receive light; and not only delighted in beholding the variety
of things, and vicissitudes of times, but raised also to find out
and discern the ordinances and decrees, which throughout all
these changes, are infallibly observed." Martineau's account of
her travels in *Eastern Life* is marked throughout by the delight
she takes in "the variety of things, and vicissitudes of times"

and the resulting style is buoyant and spirited. Yet each new place or incident invariably elicits some general comment. The prospect of the Nile prompts reflections on the effect of geography and climate on national character. The physical vigor of Egyptian youths leads her to call for a greater emphasis on physical well-being in British schools.

Eastern Life, like *Retrospect of Western Travel,* follows the sequence of places visited rather than a thematic division. However, when a particular event or sight touches on one of her preoccupations, the social critic rapidly takes over from the affable traveler. The section on the magician who performed for the travelers at Cairo swiftly leads to a discussion of superstition in general, while a visit to a harem provokes a commentary on the position of women in Muslim society. Despite this occasional editorializing, Martineau as Eastern traveler gives her reader the impression of an inquisitive and attentive observer who resists prejudging the social mores of the countries she visits.

Although Martineau insisted that *Eastern Life* was a simple travel book, it is very evident that, because of the way in which it provided her with a concrete medium for examining her religious beliefs more thoroughly, the journey was of enormous personal significance to her. Furthermore, the nature of the travel itself offered opportunities for solitude which she had rarely experienced before. In the *Autobiography* she points out that "I had never before had better opportunity for quiet meditation" (2:277), and she remarks that she habitually rode either in advance or at the rear of the caravan in order to be able to contemplate in solitude. She recounts how she frequently wandered away from her party, "among the clefts of the rocks, or so far along the beach as that I might sing unheard all the beloved old music which I never utter at home, in our little island where one can never get out of earshot!"[4] The deaf woman wandering off so that she might sing unheard by others is a curiously touching image. While Martineau's experience was in many ways unusual because of her deafness as well as her various eccentric personal traits, it is important to recognize that the daily experience of the Victorians with regard to solitude and privacy was very different from our own. Their world was, in general, physically quieter than ours, but was frequently very

much less private. Compared with her modern counterpart, an
unmarried middle-class woman like Martineau who was economically independent would have had relatively few opportunities
to be completely alone in a household that typically included
numerous servants and relatives. Victorian biographies reveal
that even the most antisocial writers of the period led lives
requiring a gregariousness which many modern writers and intellectuals would find a hindrance to intellectual activity. Women
were especially unlikely to be exempted from social commitments. While Carlyle and other male contemporaries were carefully guarded from intrusive social demands by watchful wives,
women writers like Martineau had to rely on their instructions
to servants to repel or defer unwelcome visitors.[5]

Again and again one senses in *Eastern Life* that, during this
journey, Martineau's mind was turned reflectively inward so
that the book has a contemplative quality almost entirely missing
from the American travel books. Consequently, she finds that
her usually acute observing eye is less alert than usual: "before
I had reached the bazaars, I was generally in a state of vexation
with myself for my carelessness about surrounding objects. I
hardly know what it is in these Eastern countries which disposes
one to reverie; but I verily thought, the whole journey through
. . . that I was losing my observing faculties—so often had I
to rouse myself, or to be roused by others, to heed what was
before my eyes" (*E,* 245). While her observations are frequently
as trenchant as those in her other writings, the reader has the
sense throughout that many of the scenes Martineau witnesses
are being stored reflexively in "my interior picture gallery"
(*E,* 146) rather than being sketched for the reader. This more
meditative mental state sometimes results in surprisingly revealing psychological insights as when she divulges how she closely
identified with Saint Theresa's desire for martyrdom in her youth
and how, later, she came to admire rather the mature Saint
Theresa who, as a practical religious administrator, reformed
the Carmelite order: "Martyrdom . . . would have been the
mere gratification of a selfish craving for spiritual safety. She
did much more for God and man by living to the age of sixty-
seven, and bringing back the true spirit into the corrupted body
of her order. Here she is—the woman of genius and determination—looking at us from out of her stiff head-gear—as true a

queen on this mountain throne as any empress who ever wore a crown" (*E,* 467). While she does not explicitly acknowledge it, the process she describes here is an excellent analogue for her own psychological and spiritual development which moved from a painful and introspective childhood and youth to an active and practical middle age in which she occupied herself with social and political concerns.

That the Eastern journey was, for her, as much a psychic as a physical journey is underlined by her sharp warning to other English travelers that the East is no adventure playground. "The man who goes to shoot crocodiles and flog Arabs and eat ostrich's eggs, and looks upon the monuments as so many strange old stone heaps" will only be bored by the journey. Only the traveler who confronts the experience, "in the spirit of study" (*E,* 58), will find it a rewarding one.

Advice to Other Eastern Travelers

Characteristically, much of Martineau's advice is of a strictly practical nature. She insists that the exigencies of travel are no excuse for slovenly dress. She not only emphasizes her efforts at ensuring that her traveling clothes are thoroughly washed, she even proposes that other women travelers should follow her example of "putting up a pair of flat-irons among her baggage. If she can also starch, it will add much to her comfort and that of her party, at a little cost of time and trouble" (*E,* 72–73). The Arab boat crews, she reports, tend to be bewildered by such a laundry regime and one group even deduced that ironing must be the English method for killing lice. She also advises travelers on appropriate clothing for desert conditions and has high praise for "what is called Levinge's bag—an inexpressible comfort. Without it, I believe I should scarcely have slept at all; but, as it was, I lay down every night absolutely secure from insects of every kind" (*E,* 296).

Largely for the benefit of other prospective travelers, she points out that the journey is not without its irritations or even dangers. She finds camel riding both irritating and very exhausting. She is exasperated that the management of part of the desert journey must be under the control of "our villainous Sheikh," especially when she discovers that the camel's obstinacy in browsing on "every twig of tamarisk and acacia" is because the Sheikh has economized by bringing no food for the camels or their drivers: "He trusted to our compassion for the feeding of the men, and to the Desert shrubs for the subsistence of the beasts" (E, 344).

On other occasions, she is exposed to some degree of personal danger. Once, when she is riding slightly apart from the caravan, she faints from a neuralgic pain and is, for a short time, quite alone in a barren area frequented by Bedouin bandits. Later they reach the monastery of St. Saba whose severe rule refused to admit "any woman within their gates, under any stress of weather or other accident" (E, 428). The gentlemen of the party are, however, handsomely accommodated in the monastery for the night while the women camp outside. Bedouin bandits have been seen in the vicinity and "One of the gentlemen advised me to take care of my watch; which I would thankfully have done, if I had known how." Martineau comments wryly on their departure the following morning: "All were glad, I believe, when the morning came, and we could ride away from flies and ants, and heat, and monks too holy to be hospitable, except to gentlemen who need it least" (E, 429). Typically, when confronted with apparent personal danger, Martineau reacts with sangfroid. Riding along the seashore near Batroun, close to Tripoli on the Lebanese coast,

two men with spears ran up to me, one on each side of my horse, and laid hold of the bridle,—one of them shaking his weapon in my face. Whether these were any of the coast robbers we had heard of, I do not know. My party were within call; but I thought there would be trouble and a scuffle if I brought our servants and these men into collision: so I twitched my rein out of their hands, laughed in their faces, and rode away. (E, 516)

Compared with other English travelers in the same locale, Martineau makes very little of the dangers of banditry. Far from fearing the remoteness and isolation, she seems to have welcomed the freedom from constraints that allowed her to sing unheard or to bathe alone in rivers or the sea or to meditate without being called on for social conversation.

Religious Views in *Eastern Travel*

Martineau's freethinking approach to Christianity provided her with a perspective on other faiths that was strikingly different from Victorian travelers with conventional Christian views. Far from regarding other religious beliefs as impious, she tended toward the view that religions shared a common aim, however different their modes of expression might be, a view she had expressed in her first writings while she was still a Christian. Consequently, she regards both Mohemmedanism and the early Egyptian polytheism with tolerance and sympathy. She finds the "defacement" of the monuments at Philoe by the superimposition of Christian images an example of the tendency of "the infirm human mind which is for ever obliterating, as far as it can, all ideas but its own" (*E,* 143). She is impatient of the complacent way in which the English, viewing the ancient Egyptian monuments in the British Museum and on their travels, declare them to be examples of "idolatry." Martineau argues eloquently that the reconstruction of a complex belief system from such fragmentary evidence is bound to be simplistic and distorted, and she wonders how the Christian religion might appear five thousand years later to "a careless traveler of another race, who should thrust a way among the buried pillars of our cathedral aisles, and look for superstition in every recess, and idolatry in every chapel; and who, lighting upon some carved fox and goose or grinning mask, should go home and declare that Christianity was made up of what was idolatrous, unideal and grotesque?" (*E,* 108). She is tolerant also of the ancient Eygptian worship of deities in animal forms and suggests that such worship was merely a misapplication of a sense of wonder at human coexistence with animals, "for all these thousands of years without having found any means of communication; without having done anything to bridge over the gulf which so separates them, that they appear mere phantoms to each other" (*E,* 173).

Throughout her travels she finds extensive evidence that elements of Christianity and Judaism were derived from more ancient religions. She also, atypically for an English traveler of the period, finds much to admire in the religion and culture of the region. She is especially impressed with the athletic grace of the Arabs and regards it as an example of their freedom from "the Christian contempt for the body" (*E,* 212). She even suggests that, in exchange for the plentiful supply of Christian missionaries to "the heathen," the heathen could send their own missionaries who could instruct the Christian English in "a grateful use of our noble natural endowment in our powers of sense and limb . . ." (*E,* 76).

Despite, or perhaps because of, her impatience with rigid Christian dogma, Martineau is most obviously intellectually and emotionally engaged in her account of her journey to sites mentioned in the Bible and in imagining biblical scenes in their original context. At Sinai, she imagines herself as a follower of Moses, and the vividness with which she is able to picture the mundane domestic concerns of such a character reminds us that she was, by the time that *Eastern Life* was written, already an established and extremely accomplished writer of fiction. On another occasion, she is struck by how faulty have been her mental impressions of the scene of the raising of Lazarus because she had always pictured a grave dug in the earth rather than a grave in the wall of a limestone cave like the reputed tomb of Lazarus at Bethany. The intensity of these impressions strike her as a profound contrast with the artificial solemnity associated with Bible reading and study: "O! how simple, how familiar, how *cheerful,* (yet all the more pathetic for that) are his teachings, when read in the presence of their illustrations, in comparison with the solemn delivery of them, cut up into verses, in our churches, and even in our family circles at home!" (*E,* 414). She is impressed most powerfully by the way in which, from such a perspective, the Bible ceases to be exotic, and she contends that much of the force of Christ's teaching arose simply from the way in which he had a gift for couching belief in familiar colloquial images. She provided an analogy for her English readers:

If Jesus were of Saxon race, and came now to reform and free our souls, his imagery would be our rural cottages and the alleys of our towns; the redbreast and the dog-rose and bramble; as in Galilee they were the rock and the sand-built houses, the ravens and the lilies of the field. . . . It may sound irreverent, but it ought not to do so, to conceive of him as saying "Alas! for you, Liverpool,—alas! for you, Bristol!" and as declaring that proud Edinburgh or London should be humbled. (*E,* 471)

Compared with her own intense response, she finds the tendency of other travelers to kowtow slavishly to a literal reading of biblical texts immensely irritating. She is contemptuous of those who are "enslaved by a timid and superstitious regard to the wording of the records." Her own view is that human history as a whole, rather than scriptural text, "is truly the Word of God" (*E,* 385) and thus she finds the enslavement of the timid to the Bible more offensive than the commonly denounced idolatry she encounters at the various holy sites. She is more amused than shocked by the transparent fraudulence of relics displayed at such places as the Church of the Holy Sepulchre at Jerusalem, and simply avoids the ceremony of washing the Pilgrims' feet, content to accept the description of one of her friends that "it was like a holiday in hell" (*E,* 411).

Response to Antiquities

Her response to pre-Christian antiquities is less emotionally complex, but nonetheless intensely absorbed, requiring her to reflect on the way in which Egyptian archeological evidence serves to undermine the then popular notion that the human race had only existed for six thousand years. Visiting Egypt, as she did, at a time before archeologists had uncovered many of the monuments now on open display to travelers, she did not, like so many of her contemporaries, regard the antiquities merely as picturesque ruins. She evidently itched to uncover them so that they could be viewed in something like their original state. She longs for "a great winnowing fan, such as would, without injury to human eyes and lungs, blow away the sand which buries the monuments of Egypt" (*E,* 45), but concedes that such exposure might be premature. Later, at Beyt-el-Welle she sees where a trickle of water has cleaned some of the dirt and mold from the ancient murals and is "irresistably tempted to try to cleanse a bit of the wall, and restore to sight some of its ancient paintings." Having first ascertained that "no colour would come off" she and her Arab attendant, Hasan, set to work scrubbing with soap and water, and she is regretful that time does not allow her to stay "to clean the entire temple" (*E*, 132–33). She plainly feels proud of this rather naive work of restoration and hopes that subsequent travelers may follow her example.

The central event for the tourist in Egypt was and is the visit to the Sphinx and the Great Pyramid. Martineau is so intent on the Pyramid that she passes by the Sphinx without noticing it, taking it for "a capriciously formed rock" (*E*, 217). The Pyramid itself, however, more than fulfills her expectations. She finds the ascent of the Pyramid immensely absorbing, so much so that she converses normally with her companions, hearing their replies "perfectly," and only remembers some three and a half hours later, when she sees her ear trumpet in the hands of her Arab attendant, that she has been without it the whole time. "A stronger proof could not be offered," she concludes, "of the engrossing interest of the visit to the Pyramid" (*E*, 218). Quite apart from speculation about the precise nature and causes of Martineau's deafness that this incident provokes, it underlines her oddly abstracted mental state during her Eastern tour.

Eastern Social Life and Institutions

Throughout *Eastern Life*, Martineau's comments on social life and institutions are considerably less judgmental than her assessments of their American counterparts. Here she is tentative and cautious in her remarks, while in the American books she is willing to make summary judgments based on her impressions. In *Society in America* and in *Retrospect of Western Travel* as well as elsewhere in her writings, she shows that she shares the conventional Victorian belief in the phenomenon of "national character" but in *Eastern Life*, while she suggests that the Egyptian character must have been influenced by the necessity for "perpetual vigilance against the desert" (*E*, 47), she is reluctant to generalize about what the most salient features of such a character may be.

Typically, she derives some of her most significant impressions of the qualities of Eastern culture from her observations of childrearing and of children's behavior. When she describes

visiting a harem it is clear that she regards the situation of children growing up in such a context as an eminently undesirable
one. Elsewhere in the East, however, she is impressed by the
physical grace of the children. The spontaneity of their social
behavior prompts her to lament the repression of natural expres-
sive behavior in English children. On one occasion, she divides
an orange among a group of children: One of them, "on obtaining a smile from her mother, came to me, and most gracefully
kissed my hand. This was not like an English child. Whenever
I have traveled abroad, I have wished that we could, in the
training of children, cease to interfere with natural language
in the way we do" (*E,* 507).

Surprisingly, given her outspoken statements about slavery
in America, Martineau is reticent about the same institution
in the East, reserving her particular contempt for the sexual
slavery of the harem. At the outset of her chapter on the harem,
Martineau asserts her intent of keeping an open mind on the
subject of polygamy, but declares that, after observing polygamy
as practiced in Egypt, she is able to declare it "a hell upon
earth" (*E,* 260). She feels that visiting a London slum, "the
worst room in the Rookery of St. Giles' would have affected
me less painfully" (*E,* 264). She contends that polygamy and
slavery in Egypt interact to form a "double institution" involving
the enslavement of Nubian girls as harem wives and Nubian
boys as harem guards. She regards slavery as thus practiced as
doubly iniquitous since it involves none of the responsibilities
of proprietorship: "virtual slavery is indispensably required by
the practice of polygamy; virtual proprietorship of the women
involved, without the obligations imposed by actual proprietorship; and cruel oppression of the men who should have been
husbands of these women" (*E,* 266). Unlike other travelers
observing the same institution, she does not regard polygamy
combined with slavery as solely the responsibility of its Muslim
practitioners, but is at pains to point out that Christians, too,
are implicated because the harem slaves are provided by "the
Christians of Asyoot" (*E,* 265).

Despite the intensity of her own objections, she recognizes
that the harem is a deeply entrenched institution and she observes that the women in the harem genuinely pity independent
European women, "that we had to go about traveling, and ap-

pearing in the streets without being properly taken care of,—
that is, watched. They think us strangely neglected in being
left so free, and boast of their spy system and imprisonment
as tokens of the value in which they are held" (*E, 263*). Typically, it is the vapidity and idleness of harem life which most
irritates and distresses Martineau. After Mrs. Yates's comically
futile attempts to explain to the harem women Martineau's occupation as a writer, the latter comments in exasperation, "There
is nothing about which the inmates of harems seem to be so
utterly stupid as about women having anything to do" (*E, 269*).
Unlike many of her contemporaries, Martineau is unconcerned
with the sexual dimension of harem life and is rather, throughout
her account, in a state of ferment about the idleness and vacuity
of such an existence. Because the harem inmates cannot conceive
of women having anything to occupy their time, they dawdle
as long as possible over all social exchanges in order to prolong
the entertainment of the visit of the European ladies, so that
Martineau is compelled, much against her habitual nature, to
"sit hour after hour on the deewan, without any exchange of
ideas" (*E, 263*). The physical inertia of the women's sedentary
lives is almost as distressing to her as their intellectual vapidity,
and she even suggests to an English doctor who attended several
harems "whether he could not introduce skipping ropes" (*E,
269*). The picture conjured up is an astonishing one, and unfor-
tunately, Dr. Thompson's reply is not recorded.

Despite her contempt for the institution it represents and
the idiosyncracies of her response, Martineau's reaction to both
her visits to harems is frank and direct, and, as always, she
responds spontaneously to individuals. She is given some roses
as "a farewell token" by the chief wife of one harem and comments, "I kept those roses, however. I shall need no reminding
of the most injured human beings I have ever seen,—the most
studiously depressed and corrupted women whose condition I
have witnessed: but I could not throw away the flowers which
so found their way into my hand as to bespeak for the wrongs
of the giver the mournful remembrance of my heart" (*E, 270*).

Chapter Three

The Popular Educator

The Tradition of Popular Educative Literature in the Early Nineteenth Century

By the time Harriet Martineau became established as a writer of note through the popularity of her *Illustrations of Political Economy,* the flood of printed material which accompanied the industrial revolution was already rapidly rising. In the previous century, the number of people who bought or even read books was extremely limited both because of the scarcity and high price of paper and because basic education was limited to a small section of the population. As the nineteenth century began, however, a mass reading public was developing as a result of the operation of complex social and economic forces. The population was becoming concentrated in large urban industrial centers which facilitated distribution of books and periodical publications. New industrial processes, such as the use of a steam driven printing press, made it possible for books and other publications to be printed more cheaply than before. Readers themselves were becoming more numerous as a result of the gradual trend toward democratization of education. Furthermore, because of the atmosphere of political ferment which marked the first half of the nineteenth century, the popular readership that was developing was characterized by an appetite for political discussion fed by a torrent of political tracts, pamphlets, and periodical journalism, of which William Cobbett's radical *Political Register* (1801–16) was one of the most widely circulated and controversial.

Accompanying the surge of political pamphlet journalism from the Chartists and other radical movements was a trend toward publications offering advice of various kinds to middle- and working-class readers. Self-help and self-improvement literature abounded. Much of this material related to domestic and agricultural management. William Cobbett's *Cottage Economy* (1821–22),[1] which was addressed to "the Labouring Classes of this Kingdom" and urged laboring families to keep their own livestock and make their own bread and beer, achieved a circulation that approached fifty thousand by 1828. Other books or pamphlets recommending similar management of small parcels of land continued to appear for most of the century. Some of these were directed at workers and derived much of their impetus from the Chartist slogan demanding "an acre of land and a cow" for everyone. Others, like the book by "two ladies" describing *Our Farm of Four Acres, and the Money we made by it*,[2] which Martineau discusses in *Health, Husbandry and Handicraft*, urged small-scale farming as a desirable and profitable hobby for the middle class.

A large proportion of the mass of printed material that flowed from the nineteenth-century printing presses was devoted to the popularization of ideas or information that existed elsewhere in a more complex or more sophisticated form. Brougham's Society for the Diffusion of Useful Knowledge epitomized the Utilitarians' activities in this direction. The Society's principal publication, the *Penny Magazine*,[3] carried two main types of items: articles explaining the principles of political economy in an easily digestible form, and articles explaining industrial processes. In many respects Martineau's journalism throughout her whole career followed a similar bilateral pattern. As a utilitarian, albeit one at odds with many of the other utilitarian political economists, Martineau tended to have enormous faith in industrialism as a means of bringing about human happiness. As the daughter of a textile manufacturer, her utilitarian laissez-faire political theory was coupled with a belief that economic benefits to manufacturers would inevitably benefit workers and that factory legislation was an unwarrantable governmental interference. These views are implicit whenever she describes manufacturing processes and heavily explicit in the didactic *Illustrations of Political Economy* and in her Corn Law and Game Law tales as well as in her extensive political journalism.

Martineau as a Popularizer

Martineau regarded her own gifts as a writer as essentially fitting her to be a popularizer of existing ideas rather than an original thinker. In her summary of her career which she intended to serve as her obituary, she referred, for example, to her translation and condensation of Comte in the following manner:

there is no other, perhaps, which so well manifests the real character of her ability and proper direction of her influence,—as far as each went. Her original power was nothing more than was due to earnestness and intellectual clearness within a certain range. With small imaginative and suggestive powers, and therefore nothing approaching to genius, she could see clearly what she did see, and give a clear expression to what she had to say. In short, she could popularize, while she could neither discover nor invent. (3:469)

In many respects such a description severely underestimates both Martineau's own accomplishments and the rare talents required for successful popularization.

Martineau's writings tend to draw heavily on her personal fund of experiences, and consequently she usually avoids the most serious pitfall for writers who offer advice to their readers, that of meting out suggestions in a patronizing manner. She constantly refers to anecdotes from her own life and thus provides a texture and interest in her writings on practical matters that is often absent from similar works of the period. This autobiographical component evidently afforded her some personal satisfaction. She remarks, for example, in the preface to *Health, Husbandry and Handicraft:* "It can give me nothing but pleasure to join in the endeavour to make useful these results of a long experience and observations of the homely realities of life."[4] This autobiographical element, particularly in *Health, Husbandry and Handicraft* where she dwells on her Ambleside experiences, provides closely observed incidents and commentary on domestic events, which renders the book still lively and interesting to the modern reader. Her description of her poultry yard, for example, is the careful and amused one of the intimate observer: "the favourite aversion of the drake is his own ducklings. He would destroy them every one if we did not separate them from their passionate parent. The whole feathered colony is, at times, so like the Irish quarter of a port town, with its brawls and faction fights, that imprisonment or banishment is occasionally necessary, on the one hand, and an accident-ward for victims on the other" (*H,* 291).

In many respects the way in which so much of Martineau's popular writing is rooted so directly in her own experience is reminiscent of Cobbett. Their political views, of course, diverged sharply, but it is evident that Martineau admired Cobbett's writing. They both generalize freely from their own experience and express themselves in a trenchant, emphatic manner. While they are both unabashedly opinionated, Cobbett tends to be more choleric and irascible as if he constantly pictures his reader as an imaginary political adversary. Martineau, however, gives the impression of confidently assuming that any rational reader will inevitably be persuaded to agree with her position.

Household Education

The chapters which make up *Household Education* (1849) had been written by Martineau over a period of several years as separate articles for the *People's Journal*. In *Household Education* she organized them to track the individual's educational needs and experiences from birth through maturity and old age with such titles as "The New Comer," "Intellectual Training," and "Care of the Powers." From a literary point of view, the main interest in her approach lies in the way in which she generalizes from her own subjective experience, framing each of her educational precepts with an anecdote from her own early life realized in minute detail. Thus the thread of her own experience acts as the unifying principle in what would otherwise be a collection of random essays on a common theme.

In many respects, the range of Martineau's journalistic essays provides us with an extensive map of the intellectual landscape of the period. *Household Education* reflects the way in which a larger middle-class population and the extension of formal education, as well as other more complex social and cultural causes, was both prolonging the period of early life defined as "childhood" and helping to create a greater interest in child development. Publication of works on educational theory had been escalating steadily ever since Rousseau's *Emile* (1762)[5] had provoked heated philosophical discussion of the subject in the previous century. Martineau's book was not intended to make a contribution to the philosophical debate about the ideal mode of childrearing, but rather to outline what she saw as sound principles of education and to offer practical advice to parents of all classes. To judge from her passing references in her *Autobiography,* she herself did not regard the book as a major work, although it was to become one of the most frequently reprinted of all her publications.

Compared with much of the extant Victorian material on childrearing and education, Martineau's notions of the ideal family tend to be more egalitarian than the heirarchical authoritarian model presented in many nineteenth-century sources. She stresses throughout that education should be perceived as a process that does not end in adulthood, and that "every member of the family above the yearling infant must be a member of the domestic school of mutual instruction, and must know that he is so."[6] She is emphatic that education or training which is merely imposed is of no value: "Every member of the household,—children, servants, apprentices,—every inmate of the dwelling, must have a share in the family plan, or those who make it are despots and those who are excluded are slaves" (*HE,* 10).

Although, like most Victorians, Martineau clearly expected young children to develop considerable powers of self-control, she thought that there was little purpose served in trying to develop self-discipline by forcible means: "There is a tyranny in making a lively child sit on a high stool with nothing to do, even though the thing is ordained for its own good; and every child has a keen sense of tyranny. The patience taught by such means cannot be thorough; it cannot be an amiable and cheerful patience, pervading the whole temper" (*HE,* 126). Similarly, she saw no purpose in rigidly censoring a child's reading by providing bowdlerized versions of the classics: "Whatever children do not understand slips through the mind and leaves no trace; and what they do understand of matters of passion is to them divested of mischief. Purified editions of noble books are monuments of wasted labor . . ." (*HE,* 257).

Martineau was sometimes circumspect about expressing her views on women's rights if she felt that the forum was inappropriate, but in *Household Education* she asserts firmly that girls have the same right to an intellectual education as boys. She is incredulous about the way in which many works on education, which

she otherwise admires, complacently and contradictorily argue
against education for girls: "we find it taken for granted that
girls are not to learn the dead languages and mathematics, because they are not to exercise professions where these attain-
ments are wanted; and a little further on we find it said that
the chief reason for boys and young men studying these things
is to improve the quality of their minds" (*HE,* 271). Characteristically, she evidently feels that, having exposed the illogicality
of her opponents' argument, nothing more need be said on
the matter.

In her travel books, Martineau observed that both Arab children in Egypt and the children of settlers in America developed
impressive physical competence and grace compared with their
English counterparts. In *Household Education* she argues in favor
of a program of physical as well as intellectual education, citing,
typically, an earnestly presented, but absurdly exaggerated, example:

Look at the pale student, who lives shut up in his study, never having
been trained to use his arms and hands but for dressing and feeding
himself, turning over his books, and guiding the pen. Look at his
spindles of arms and his thin fingers, and compare them with the
brawny limbs of the blacksmith or the hands of the quay-porter, whose
grasp is like that of a piece of strong machinery. Compare the feeble
and awkward touch of the bookworm, who can hardly button his
waistcoat or carry his cup of tea to his mouth, with the power that
the modeller, the ivory-carver, and the watch-maker have over their
fingers. It is education which has made the difference between these.
(*HE,* 31–32)

The assumption behind all the notions about education presented in Martineau's books is that most children will never
attend school. Although more and more children were receiving
formal schooling for longer periods as the century progressed,
Martineau's assumption was, for most middle-class female children and nearly all the children of working-class parents, substantially correct. Even children who did go to school generally
attended either intermittently or for a very short time. The
main emphasis of *Household Education,* therefore, is on the education received by children at home, though Martineau takes pains
to stress that the home, even with the provision of well-qualified

tutors, cannot compete with the school in teaching "book-knowledge" (*HE,* 214).

The central interest of *Household Education,* for the student of Martineau's work, is not so much in her educational theory itself as in the way in which the book clearly served as something of a dress rehearsal for the more systematic personal reminiscence of the *Autobiography.* Many incidents from her own childhood are presented in the first person; others are more or less disguised by third-person narration. In some cases, as in the account she provides of parental insensitivity to the onset of deafness, the third-person disguise may have seemed necessary, both because the account was still painful and because she is portraying her parents' attitude as implicitly tyrannical:

I have known deafness grow upon a sensitive child so gradually as never to bring the moment when her parents felt impelled to seek her confidence; and the moment therefore never arrived. She became gradually borne down in health and spirits by the pressure of her trouble, her springs of pleasure all poisoned, her temper irritated and rendered morose, her intellectual pride puffed up to an insufferable haughtiness, and her conscience brought by perpetual pain of heart into a state of trembling soreness,—all this, without one word ever being offered to her by any person whatever of sympathy or sorrow about her misfortune. (*HE,* 148)

Yet other incidents less highly charged with feeling or which do not reflect on her parents are also narrated in the third person with a similar "I knew a little girl . . ." formula.

The often heavy-handed prescriptive tone of *Household Education* is effectively leavened by Martineau's use of these accounts. At times these are more or less incidental to the argument, as is the case when she describes the intensity of her own sensory experiences as a child: "I tried to walk round a tree (an elm, I believe), clasping the tree with both arms; and nothing that has happened today is more vivid to me than the feel of the rough bark to the palms of my hands and the entanglement of the grass to my feet. And then at night there was the fearful wonder at the feel of the coarse calico sheets, and at the creaking of the turn-up bedstead when I moved" (*HE,* 229). The intensity of the remembered sensation tends to evoke empathy and effectively prevents the reader from objectifying the child. This is particularly the case when she frankly reveals the idiosyncratic nature of her childhood fears:

Some of my worst fears in infancy were from lights and shadows. The lamplighter's torch on a winter's afternoon, as he ran along the street, used to cast a gleam, and the shadows of the window-frames on the ceiling; and my blood ran cold at the sight, every day, even though I was on my father's knee, or on the rug in the middle of the circle round the fire. Nothing but compulsion could make me enter our drawing-room before breakfast on a summer morning; and if carried there by the maid, I hid my face in a chair that I might not see what was dancing on the wall. If the sun shone, as it did at that time of day, on the glass lustres on the mantel-piece, fragments of gay color were cast on the wall; and as they danced when the glass drops were shaken, I thought they were alive,—a sort of imps. But as I never told anybody what I felt, these fears could not be met, or charmed away; and I grew up to an age which I will not mention before I could look steadily at prismatic colors dancing on the wall. (*HE,* 115–16)

From Charlotte Brontë's remarks about her own deeply felt response to *Household Education* and from its enormous popularity among its contemporary audience, we may surmise that many nineteenth-century readers saw the book as more than merely another text providing educational advice. Like Brontë, many other readers may well have read her account of the needless cruelties inflicted on children in the name of parental discipline and "firmness" with an all-too-familiar sense of their own childhood brought to mind.

Health, Husbandry and Handicraft

In many respects *Health, Husbandry and Handicraft* (1861) is an obvious miscellany without the strong autobiographical thread which serves to unify *Household Education.* The section on "Health," for example, enumerates the health hazards of various occupations with chapters on "The Rural Labourer," "The Baker," "The Governess," and so on, but other chapters dwell on such topics as suicide, the cost of cottage construction, and diet. While all of these might cohere well enough with the chapters on domestic management in the "Husbandry" section, the final section on "Handicraft" is simply a collection of Martineau's articles on various types of factories such as the Birmingham glass works and the bobbin mill at Ambleside. In most of these, Martineau is characteristically entranced with industrial processes and adopts a blandly enthusiastic tone, out of keeping with the two earlier sections. The only common thread that runs through all three sections is Martineau's intense interest in thrifty and efficient practical management, which she extolled as the supreme virtue of domestic life as well as a desirable goal for institutions, industry, and the nation as a whole.

Her emphasis on reform in diet and dress in the section on health prefigures the movement for "rational" dress and diet which had an extensive influence at the end of the nineteenth century. In chapter after chapter she stresses that the high rates of both infant and early adult mortality could easily be reduced by simple means. Characteristically, as a lifetime proponent of economic individualism, she places little stress on government responsibility for public health but suggests that individual households can remedy ill-health independently.

She devotes extensive space to the high rates of infant mortality under the succinct and almost Shavian title, "Herod in the Nineteenth Century." Herself a victim of the practice of putting babies from middle-class families out to wet nurses, she speaks feelingly on the custom as a cause of sickness among the children of the wealthy as well as of the frequent deaths of babies whose mothers became wet nurses to earn money. She extends her analysis of the causes of infant mortality beyond the aspects of health and nutrition to social conditions. In the chapter headed "A Death Watch Worth Dreading" she attacks, as a primary cause of infanticide, the institution of burial societies through which parents whose child died received a cash settlement to cover funeral expenses. With characteristic intense but limited vision, she advocates legislation to require burial societies to operate under the same regulations as life insurance companies, recommends vaccination of infants, and attacks the custom of employing wet nurses. She does not stress the connection between poverty and infant mortality rates or see poverty itself as the main cause of infanticide.

Despite her inability to taste or smell, which seems to have originated in the same damage to her nervous system that caused her deafness, Martineau evidently relished good food and placed great importance on its proper preparation and cooking. She speaks feelingly against the practice of forcing children to eat food they dislike. Using the same sort of transparent third-person disguise as in *Household Education,* she recalls her own experience of being forced to drink milk: "I have seen a pale-faced little girl, with lead-coloured circles round her eyes, compelled to take milk breakfasts till she was 'of the proper age' to have coffee, and enduring, in consequence, a whole youth of indigestion. She did not dislike milk; but she could not digest it; and during her entire childhood, she went to her lessons with a suffocating lump in her throat, and a head full of pain or noises" (*H,* 19).

Martineau's notions of food reform differ noticeably from those of food reformers later in the century who had begun to approach nutrition as a science and were critical of the traditional pattern of diet. Instead, she idealizes the diet of several centuries earlier, recommending the "beef and manchet" diet of "Queen Elizabeth's time." Similarly, she recommends a return to the old-fashioned daily schedule of eating a main meal of the day at two in the afternoon and she argues against the "modern" fashion of having a large meal in the evening.

A movement for "rational dress" for women had existed for some time and had attracted a number of adherents, particularly in America, "by women who refused the inconvenience of Paris fashions in American homesteads" (*H,* 59). Martineau was angry at the scorn poured on the rational dress movement and particularly on the bloomer costume by the English caricaturists. She found the women's fashions of mid-century somewhat less absurd and damaging to the health than that of a few decades before which had involved tight-lacing, multiple layers of skirts, and petticoats which acted as a fire hazard, as well as the extensive use of poisonous chemicals in cosmetics. Nevertheless, she observed that contemporary women's dress performed few of the essential functions of clothing, protecting the wearer from neither "cold, heat, damp or glare." The extremes of fashion were always absurd and were sometimes positively dangerous. She wrote of accidents in which children were "swept off pathways, or foot-bridges, or steamboat decks by the pitiless crinoline, or hoops of some unconscious walking balloon!" (*H,* 58). She was preeminently scornful of the ridiculous appearance of women physically incapacitated by their fashionable clothes, "A woman on a sofa looks like a child popping up from a haycock" (*H,* 57). The image of the Victorian woman comically impeded from almost any physical activity by her fashionable clothing was a familiar target of *Punch* cartoons of the day. Despite her scorn, unlike the *Punch* cartoonists, Martineau is clearly aware of the intensity of the social pressure on women to dress fashionably and consequently her derision is reserved more for the costume itself than for the women who succumbed to the demands of fashion.

Basing most of her ideas on her experience of organizing a building society to construct workers' cottages at Ambleside, she advocates well-built, adequately drained, and ventilated housing for workers in towns and attacks the cheaply built unhealthy houses that were erupting everywhere in the rapidly expanding towns in order to accommodate the huge numbers of factory operatives. As always, she regards education about housing and health as the solution to the problem through the way in which it could bring about a change in attitudes. She never suggests that the exploitative inadequate housing provided for workers was an inevitable by-product of the economic system she admired.

Throughout her writings and, most noticeably, in works such as *Household Education* and *Health, Husbandry and Handicraft,* Martineau puts her faith in education as a means of social change. She attacks irrational traditional beliefs, which she thought were detrimental to childrearing, especially when parents carried their superstitions to such extremes as refusing to wash a baby's arms for the first six months in the belief that this would prevent thieving in later life. She placed enormous faith in education as a means of furthering the cause of better public health. Physical fitness for young women could, she thought, be taught by means of swimming lessons. Inspired by an advertisement for swimming lessons in Marylebone by "an efficient female teacher," she wonders about the possibility of spreading swimming training widely: "There are multitudes of young women on the look out for means of honest subsistence. Why should

not teachers at Public Baths instruct ten, or twelve, or twenty
strong and willing girls to swim, in order to teach others to
swim?" (*H,* 23).

Optimistic as ever, she thought that public ignorance and
carelessness in the matter of food preparation could be
countered by traveling teachers of cooking: "Let half a dozen
popular teachers like Soyer (but who *is* like him!) travel through
the country, each with a portable kitchen, and show all the
women and girls in town and country the best way to make
and cook the common preparations of food; and the benefit
will be equal to a rise of wages to the labouring man at once.
The mere secret of the stew—now rarely or ever seen on the
cottage table—would be as good as another shilling a-week in
health and strength" (*H,* 37). She evidently found the ignorance
of many women about food and cookery nothing short of bewil-
dering: "We have seen ladies buying pork under a sweltering
summer sun, and inquiring for geese in January and July, and
taking up with skinny rabbits in May and letting the season of
mackerel, herrings, salmon, and all manner of fish pass over
unused" (*H,* 33). Oddly enough, it does not occur to her that
this ignorance was principally the result of the population as a
whole becoming more urbanized and therefore, unfamiliar with
the seasonal availability and quality of different foods.

The liveliest part of *Health, Husbandry and Handicraft* is Martineau's description of her Ambleside establishment, which was
published separately under the title *Our Farm of Two Acres.*[7]
In many respects her project of raising food for her own household was at odds with the principles of political economy that
she had devoutly and consistently preached all her life. An individual household investing money and labor in providing for
its individual needs ran strictly against the theory of division
of labor which Martineau had promoted so enthusiastically for
rural dwellers in such tales as *Brooke and Brooke Farm* (1832).[8]
She is rather self-consciously emphatic, therefore, that the experiment arose out of necessity because "essential comforts" were
so frequently unobtainable in the neighborhood: "The supply
of milk . . . could never be depended on; and it failed when
it was most wanted—in the traveling season when the district
was thronged with strangers. During that season, even the supply
of meat was precarious. Fowls, hams, eggs, butter, everything

was precarious or unattainable; so that housekeeping was, in the guest season, a real anxiety" (*H,* 215). She is less guarded on this matter when she is discussing Cobbett and admits that she is attracted to his glowing portraits of self-sufficiency for the individual household: "I own that my heart warms to his descriptions of the cottager's wife at her bread-board and oven. He would have had everybody, even the day-labourer's wife, brew at home also; and there is something fascinating in his eloquence on behalf of meals of home-made bread, fat bacon and beer, in contrast with the potatoes he so abhorred, and wishy-washy tea" (*H,* 215). Her adherence to the principles of political economy, however, compels her to argue that such a system is essentially uneconomic since it results in "fifty cottagers' wives brewing, with their fifty sets of utensils, and at a cost of fifty days' labour, when they might get their beer more cheaply as to money, and without any expenditure of time, at the brewery" (*H,* 215).

Despite the contradiction between practice and theory, Martineau's accounts of her farming experiment in both *Household Education* and *Health, Husbandry and Handicraft* are shot through with enthusiasm and delight. She is wary of recommending small-scale husbandry as a profitable enterprise and describes a popular book of the time by "two ladies" which did so as "somewhat too tempting," but suggests that such a project as the ladies describe could be "a real boon to a class of society which sorely needs such aid: the class of gentlewomen who have not enough to do" (*H,* 270). She is evidently proud of her well-kept livestock, but is frustrated by the absence of adequate agricultural statistics and by the virtual nonexistence of veterinary medicine.

Martineau is an advocate of rural and domestic pursuits for intellectuals, less for their own sake than because it offers a balance between physical and mental life. A rural life without intellectual pursuits does not seem to her to be a desirable goal: "To have been reared in a farm-house, remote from society and books, and ignorant of everything beyond the bounds of the parish is one thing; and to pass from an indolent or a literary life in town to rural pursuits, adopted with purpose is another" (*H,* 297). Thus, unlike Cobbett, she is not promoting the return of a lost ideal agrarian age, but rather recommending outdoor pursuits as an antidote to the enervated life of those whose work committed them to the physically inert life of the middle-class urban dweller.

Popularizing Philosophy: The Translation of Comte

For a famous and established writer to devote her efforts to the translation and adaptation of another's work seems, at first sight, a curious choice of task. In her introduction to her translation and abridgment of Auguste Comte's *Philosophie Positive*[9] Martineau explains that she undertook the task in order that Comte should receive proper credit for his analysis which was already becoming widely disseminated. More importantly, she suggests, she wished to make the work more readily available to the general reader. While she thought that the French language itself could present no difficulty to the educated reader, Comte's work had originally been in the form of a series of lectures delivered intermittently over many years and thus it was frequently repetitive. Although Martineau does not suggest that it was one of her reasons for undertaking the task, we may surmise that she was also attracted to it partly because Comte's views were so controversial and were likely to anger precisely the same section of the public as had been outraged by her *Letters on the Laws of Man's Nature and Development* two years earlier, described in chapter 1. Her introduction to her translation anticipated the furore in a faintly triumphant tone: "the enmity of the religious world to the book will not slacken for its appearing among us in an English version. . . . The theological world can not but hate a book which treats of theological belief as a transient state of the human mind. . . . As M. Comte treats of theology and metaphysics as destined to pass away, theologians and metaphysicians must necessarily abhor, dread, and despise his work."[10]

However attractive or worthwhile the task of such a translation, it was an onerous undertaking. She condensed the six volumes of Comte's original book into a single one, which required her to work enormously long hours, sometimes translating and condensing as many as forty or fifty pages in a single day. Despite the long hours of work and the fact that the project coincided with the summer guest season at Ambleside, Martineau evidently found the work rewarding: "I often said to myself and others, in the course of it, that I should never enjoy any thing so much again. And I believe that if I were now to live and work for twenty years, I could never enjoy any thing more" (2:390).

Martineau was not alone in her attraction to Comte's work. George Henry Lewes had summarized Comte's ideas in his *Biographical History of Philosophy*[11] in 1845 and Herbert Spencer referred to Comte in his *Social Statics,*[12] which bore some resemblance to a Comtean approach to the emerging study of social science. The reasons for Comte's attractiveness to Martineau and her contemporaries are fairly self-evident. His views on the inevitability of social evolution mirror closely the information on physical evolution that was issuing from Darwin's precursors. He also offered an all-encompassing systematic approach to the study of society. Human society, Comte argued, passed through three crucial stages of evolution. The first, the theocratic stage, had evolved to monotheism, having passed through the earlier stages of fetishism and polytheism. The second, the "metaphysical," stage was characterized by the search for explanations and causes. The ultimate stage of human society was the "positive" in which human beings would come to understand their world through empirical observation of phenomena. Comte's system provided a broader and more intellectually coherent context for Martineau's necessarian views than Atkinson's rag-bag of amateur science. The notion of cultural evolution from theism to empiricism which Comte delineated provided reassurance that her views had the force of historical inevitability on their side while those of her detractors were simply anachronistic: "While the disciples of dogma are living in a magic cavern, painted with wonderful shows, and the metaphysical philosophers are wandering in an enchanted wood, all tangle and bewilderment, the positive philosophers have emerged upon the broad, airy, sunny common of nature, with firm ground underfoot and unfathomable light overhead" (3:325).

Despite the way in which Martineau was strongly attracted to the systematic method, it is interesting to note that much in Comte's philosophy is in sharp opposition to her most strongly held views. Comte was evidently a firm believer in the superior-

ity of the white races and he also argued emphatically that
women were inferior to men and suited only for domestic life.
Curiously, Martineau never comments on these discrepancies
between her world view and Comte's. Nor does she remark
on Comte's essentially hierarchical view of the world; whereas
Martineau might have wished to replace the hierarchy of the
Catholic church with a democratic republic, Comte proposed,
instead, a secular hierarchy headed by a technocratic elite. In
part this puzzling absence of comment on the aspects of Comte's
theory that stood in sharp contradiction to her own views is,
quite simply, as Webb[13] points out in his biography, another
example of Martineau's lack of critical ability. She was, above
all, an enthusiast, and was quite as willing to allow Comte's
antithetical opinions to pass her by as she had been to ignore
Atkinson's fuzzy thinking and muddleheaded scholarship.

Popular Histories: *The History of the Peace* and *British Rule in India*

Much of Martineau's writing, particularly her diverse journalism, *Illustrations of Political Economy,* and *Autobiography* provides
us with extraordinarily valuable source material for an understanding of the cultural and political history of the period. In
some of these writings, especially in her *Daily News* articles
and *Autobiography,* it is plain that she was conscious of recording
the events of her own times for future readers. At times, such
documentation had a palpable political purpose, as when she
produced *England and her Soldiers* (1859) based on information
provided by Florence Nightingale about the calamitous misman-
agement of army supplies during the Crimean War. Although
Florence Nightingale herself was a skillful propagandist, she
evidently recognized that Martineau's eye for detail and anecdote could sharpen her own firsthand account of War Office
incompetence into a powerful political tool.

This unabashed sense of purpose is largely missing from the
more formal historical accounts of the *History of the Peace*
(1849)[14] and *British Rule in India* (1857).[15] The *History of the
Peace* was commissioned by Charles Knight whose publication
of a wide range of books and periodicals intended to inform

the growing number of the newly literate was a major phenomenon of nineteenth-century publishing. Knight produced the work in a series of thirty monthly numbers and then published it as a two-volume book in 1849. The work is a significant monument, both to Knight's shrewdness and enterprise as a publisher and to Martineau's extraordinary industry and her ability to render historical events in a cogent and intelligible form. Writing the history of the first half of her own century required the digestion of a flood of print even more diverse than the torrent of parliamentary blue books and similar publications on which she had relied for the background material for her *Illustrations of Political Economy.*

The work had been begun by Knight himself in 1846 in a mood of optimism about the reforms and economic expansion he had witnessed in the first half of the century. Increased business responsibilities prevented him from continuing, and he turned the work over to G. L. Craik who died after completing only a few chapters. Knight then offered the completion of the *History* to Martineau who, after some hesitation, accepted.

The scope of the *History* was originally planned to cover the period between the Battle of Waterloo in 1815 and the repeal of the Corn Laws in 1846. Knight's and Craik's contributions had covered only the first five years and Martineau's responsibility for the *History* began with the year 1820. Later, when the work had achieved popular success, she completed an introductory volume to cover the period from 1800 to 1815. When the work was republished in America she contributed a concluding chapter to bring the *History* to the beginning of the Crimean War in 1854.

Although it was not part of Knight's intention for Martineau to produce an account of the period with the object of attempting to prove the validity of her political and economic views, the *History of the Peace* gives strictly a laissez-fairist's interpretation of the period. She is willing to argue a dogmatic laissez-faire position even in such areas as factory legislation where most of her fellow theorists were inclined to compromise. Throughout the two volumes Martineau consistently pins her faith on the twin solutions of education and an extended suffrage as a means of social improvement and accords little significance to reformist legislation: "Either the people must be governed without partici-

pation from themselves—that is England must go back into despotism; or the people must be educated into a capacity for being
governed by themselves, through the principle of representa-
tion. The only possible education for political, as for all other
moral duty, is by the exercise of the duty itself."[16]

Despite its obvious bias, Martineau's *History of the Peace* remains an important text for reaching an understanding of the
complex social and political movements that shaped the events
of the first half of the nineteenth century. It is worth noting
that even as distinguished an historian as Elie Halévy used Martineau's history as a major source for his own important history
of England in the nineteenth century.[17]

British Rule in India, which was published during the Indian
Mutiny, is a surprisingly cogent account of British domination
over "that remote, and odd, and troublesome settlement of
ours."[18] It was written principally as a result of Florence Nightingale's influence and began, not as an attempt to provide a formal
history, but as a series of articles on India in the *Daily News.*
While she did not question the right of the British to govern
India as a colonial possession, she places an unusually high value,
for a British writer of the period, on the importance of understanding Indian culture and customs. Repeatedly she defends
the East India Company because of their direct knowledge of
Indian affairs and distrusts both the London administrators of
the Company and the even more remote government advisors
in Whitehall.

Perhaps the most apt adjective for Martineau as an historian
is "Churchillean." Like Winston Churchill, she has an acute
sense both of anecdote and of the memorable rhetorical phrase;
but, like his history of World War II, her histories, both of
British rule in India and of domestic history during the first
half of the nineteenth century, are marked by a sharp and un-
swerving personal bias.

Martineau as a Journalist

The twentieth-century distinction between the status and function of a "writer" and that of a "journalist" was rarely made
in the literary world of the nineteenth century. The majority
of the writers who are now regarded as significant literary figures

had some connection with the journalism of their day. George Eliot, Dickens, and Thackeray, for example, all wrote extensively for periodical publications ranging respectively from the serious-minded *Westminster Review,* to the popular *Household Words,* which was aimed at a middle-class, middlebrow audience, to *Punch,* whose cartoons and comic sketches mirrored the views of an educated middle-class audience. Any writer of the period intending to earn a living solely from writing almost inevitably relied on publication in the periodical press as a financial mainstay. Martineau, who had supported herself and her dependents entirely on the proceeds of her writing ever since the publication of *Illustrations of Political Economy,* was no exception. She published articles in such publications as the *People's Journal,* the *Leader,* the *Edinburgh Review, Cornhill Magazine, Once a Week,* the *Westminster Review,* as well as over sixteen hundred articles in the *Daily News.*

Martineau's articles in the *Daily News* commented on current political events but also gave her an opportunity to discuss the implications of her views on such subjects as the abolition of slavery and the state of women's rights. In both cases she based her explicit arguments largely on economic rather than ethical grounds, even though we may surmise that the impetus for her argument in each case arose from a sense of moral outrage. Many of her discussions of the vicissitudes of the cotton industry stress the folly of relying on the production of slavery and urged the cotton manufacturers to develop sources of supply based on free labor. Similarly, in her articles on women and employment in the *Daily News* and elsewhere, she quoted statistics to show that the vast majority of women who were employed worked strictly because of the necessity of supporting themselves and their dependents. Drawing on police statistics she exposed the extent of physical abuse of women and children and argued that this arose from the way in which both were assigned a subordinate and degraded social role.

Some of Martineau's most interesting journalistic essays were the obituaries she prepared for the *Daily News.* These were collected in *Biographical Sketches*[19] in order to aid her finances when her investments were no longer yielding an adequate income. Her necessarian convictions and Comtean philosophy give her a view of history as evolutionary inevitability, only margin-

ally affected by the activities of individuals. Thus, she tended
to portray her contemporaries either as "characters" or as observers and interpreters of historical events rather than as origi-
nators of political and social movements. Her sketch of Robert
Owen is an interesting case in point. Even allowing for the
fact that he had developed views on factory reform in particular
and on society in general that were in sharp contrast to Martineau's rigid laissez-faire dogma, she devotes amazingly little
space to his theory and tends to treat his views as merely idiosyncratic and irrational: "always a gentle bore in regard to his
dogmas and his expectations; always palpably right in his descriptions of human misery; always thinking he had proved a thing
when he had asserted it, in the force of his own conviction;
and always really meaning something more rational than he
had actually expressed. It was said by way of mockery that he
might live in parallelograms, but he argued in circles; but this
is rather too favourable a description of one who did not argue
at all, nor know what argument meant" (B, 313). Allowing
that Owen's character and manner may well have been much
as Martineau describes them, her account is extraordinary in
that it ignores the enormous effect Owen had as an early socialist
and as a founder of the cooperative movement.

Her ability to characterize her subject succinctly is at its best
when she is describing those of little or no significance on the
political scene. Her accounts of literary characters are remarkable records of the period. She is particularly fascinated with
the lives of figures who had presided over several generations
of literary life. She writes an especially warm account of one
of the Miss Berrys who had been a notable saloniste from Dr.
Johnson's day until her death in 1852. Martineau is especially
intrigued with the perspective such a long life must give to
the rise and fall of literary fashions and reputation: "The short
career of Byron passed before her eyes like a summer storm;
and that of Scott constituted a great interest of her life for many
years. What an experience—to have studied the period of hor-
rors, represented by Monk Lewis—of conventionalism in Fanny
Burney—of metaphysical fiction in Godwin—of historical romance in Scott—and of a new order of fiction in Dickens, which
is yet too soon to characterise by a phrase!" (B, 296).

The sketches are also of interest for the light they shed on

Martineau's personal evaluation of particular individuals. She does not appear to have felt constrained by the conventional pious hypocrisies of writing an obituary. Her accounts of her old enemies, Croker and Lockhart of the *Quarterly Review,* while by no means deliberately malicious, made no attempt to disguise her acrimony toward them. Rather than producing a vituperative account, she provides an analysis of the causes for both Croker and Lockhart's practice of systematically demolishing reputations as well as the *Quarterly Review*'s techniques of character assassination. Despite its obvious bias, the latter is an important record for any scholar who wished to understand the climate that nineteenth-century writers inhabited. She diagnoses Lockhart's behavior as the result of "moral obtuseness" but devotes more attention to Croker whose relish in hatcheting writers in the *Quarterly* was already notorious enough for Macaulay to remark of him: "Croker is a man who would go a hundred miles through sleet and snow, on the top of a coach, in a December night, to search a parish register, for the sake of showing that a man is illegitimate, or a woman older than she says she is" (*B*, 378). Martineau suggests that Croker's "malignant ulcer of the mind" resulted from his disappointment with his mediocre political career and suggests that this mediocrity itself arose from the want of "heart" that prevented him from making the best use of moderate talents: "It was the heart element that was amiss. A good heart has wonderful efficacy in making moderate talent available. Where heart is absent, the most brilliant abilities fail, as is said in such cases, 'unaccountably' " (*B*, 383).

The *Biographical Sketches* are, almost without exception, spirited and eccentric in very much the same manner as the *Autobiography.* Despite their origins in a publication as ephemeral as a daily newspaper, they provide a vital record of a segment of nineteenth-century social and literary life.

Martineau contributed numerous articles to Dickens's popular periodical, *Household Words.* Her contributions fall into two main areas of recurring interest to her: the description of various new industrial processes; and discussions of education, particularly the education of the handicapped, with an analysis of the ways in which the mentally or physically handicapped can best be integrated and accommodated in society at large in such articles as "Three Graces of Christian Science"[20] and

"Blindness."[21] Compared with the maudlin sentimentality that surrounds much nineteenth-century writing on the subject of physical disability, Martineau's treatment of the subject is both frank and sensitive. She gives thoughtful consideration to the minute particulars of overcoming the educational handicaps of the deaf and the blind. She also reflects at length on the difficulties faced by the parents of handicapped children and advises against the self-immolation of parents in the care of a disabled child, advice which ran strictly counter to the popular Victorian view of the crippled, or otherwise disabled, child as an opportunity for meritorious self-sacrifice on the part of its parent: "If it were good that a mother should nurse an infirm child through the day and guard it all the night, that she should devote all her time and all her love, and sacrifice all her pleasures to it, and minister to its wishes every hour of its life,—if it were good that she should do this, it would not be enough. It is not good, and it is not enough" (*HE,* 133). Even more strikingly, under the bald title "Idiots Again" she describes a mother's gradual realization that her child is "mentally defective":

As the weeks pass, however, and still the child takes no notice, a sick misgiving sometimes enters the mother's mind—a dread of she does not know what, but it does not last long. You may trust a mother for finding out charms and promise of some sort or other in her baby—be it what it may. Time goes on; and the singularity is apparent that the baby makes *no response* to anything. He is not deaf . . . His mother longs to feel the clasp of his arms round her neck; but her fondlings receive no return. His arm hangs lax over her shoulder. She longs for a look from him, and lays him back in her lap, hoping that they may look into each others' eyes; but he looks at nobody. All his life long nobody will ever meet his eyes, and neither in that way nor in any other way will his mind expressly meet that of anybody else.[22]

What makes such a passage affecting, even to the modern reader who approaches it equipped with a different set of attitudes, is that rather than relying on a deliberately pathetic rendering of a subject which is already full of pathos, Martineau chooses instead a rather cool and patient account of the precise stages of the mother's rationalizations.

After having been a major contributor to *Household Words,*

Martineau finally discontinued her association with the journal in 1853. She had been dissatisfied with Dickens's editorship for some time. He tended to be high-handed and opinionated and would cut or rewrite parts of his authors' submissions to an extent unusual even for the editorial practices of the day. Mrs. Gaskell was especially annoyed with his lordly interventions in her pieces. Draconian editing of this kind was much more common in nineteenth-century periodical publications than it is today, in part because so many journals did not reveal the authorship of articles and thus tended to adhere to a "house style" in their approach. As a veteran journalist, Martineau seems to have accepted Dickens's dictatorial editing with good grace, but she became increasingly impatient with his attitudes and the tone which *Household Words* adopted on some of the issues in which she took a serious interest. When it was proposed in 1849 that she contribute a series on "the employment of women," she declined on the grounds that "every contribution of the kind was necessarily excluded by Mr. Dickens's prior articles on behalf of his view of Woman's position; articles in which he ignored the fact that nineteen-twentieths of the women of England earn their bread, and in which he prescribes the function of Women; viz., to dress well and look pretty, as an adornment to the homes of men" (2:419). Later in the same year, Dickens rejected her story about the Jesuit, Pere d'Estélan, because it gave too favorable a view of a Catholic. Martineau pointed out that the hero of her story lived "at a date and in a region where Romanism was the only Christianity" (2:420), but Dickens was adamant on the subject. The final break between Martineau and *Household Words* came when she came across a reprinted story, "The Yellow Mask," which had originally appeared in *Household Words*[23] and which contained some explicitly anti-Catholic statements. She wrote to Dickens's subeditor, W. H. Wills, severing her connection with the magazine. Dickens was irate at what he evidently saw as an unreasonable defection. They clashed publicly in print a year later when they disputed one another's statistics about factory accidents: Dickens, through the pages of *Household Words,* and Martineau in a pamphlet, *The Factory Controversy: A Warning Against Meddling Legislation* (1855)[24] on behalf of the manufacturers. Dickens's statistics were, almost certainly, not entirely accurate, but he argued validly enough that it was impossible "to justify, by arithmetic, a thing unjustifiable by any code of morals."[25] Martineau tenaciously clung to the laissez-faire view that the interests of workers and manufacturers were essentially the same and resisted any legislation over the safety of workers in factories as governmental "interference" in what she believed to be a free and mutually beneficial relationship. The understandably irascible Dickens concluded: "I do suppose that there never was such a wrongheaded woman born—such a vain one—or such a Humbug."[26]

Martineau's Influence on Popular Opinion

The precise influence of a literary and public figure like a Martineau or a Dickens is almost impossible to determine. Despite her retrogressive economic theory, Martineau also acted as something of a bellwether in matters of social change. Her attitudes toward slavery, secularism, and the status of women, from being outré in the extreme in the second quarter of the century, were widely held by the time of her death, although the extent to which her own writings contributed to the shift in public opinion can never be determined. She contributed a frankness to public discussion which helped offset the sentimental hypocrisy that was so frequently the hallmark of the nineteenth-century popular press. If she was in the vanguard of popular opinion on some issues, it is undeniable that in other areas she was essentially reactionary. She was intransigent about her views on political economy, and these frequently meshed with her early upbringing in a textile factory owner's family. She split statistical hairs with Dickens in order to prove to him that his crusade against accidents in factories was wrongheaded, and she even succumbed to the manufacturers' argument that adequate safety legislation would "ruin" the industry. Yet even here, where the light of subsequent events has shown her assessment of the situation to have been entirely mistaken, her polemical writing was so vigorous and so trenchantly argued that her contribution to the quality, if not the content of the debate was significant.

One way in which her influence can be gauged is the way in which all sorts of "riders of hobbies" as she called them continued to approach her all her life with the object of persuading her to write about their own preoccupations. She was constantly canvassed in this way while she was writing the *Illustrations of Political Economy* and she was similarly pressured by such figures as Florence Nightingale when she was writing editorial columns for the *Daily News*. In the case of the *Illustrations of Political Economy* there seems to be some evidence that Martineau's writing was influential to the extent that it cogently and simply expressed a particular economic theory and thus became a useful political tool for parliamentarians like Brougham. The influence of the *Daily News* editorials is somewhat harder to assess since they covered a wide range of topics rather than promoting a particular theory like the political economy tales.

Advice to "Fellow Sufferers": *Life in the Sickroom* and "Letter to the Deaf"

Martineau's writings frequently examine the problems of managing a physical disability. Some of her most convincing fiction focuses on the effect of physical disability on individual psychology. The most striking examples are the struggles of Hugh in *The Crofton Boys*[27] to overcome his own self-pity after his foot has been amputated, and the sympathetic characterization of Maria Young, the lame governess in *Deerbrook*.[28] Many of her articles on educational methods for the deaf or the blind published in *Household Words* and other periodicals offer implicit advice to the handicapped or their families, but in "Letter to the Deaf" (1834)[29] and *Life in the Sickroom* (1844)[30] she specifically addresses those who, like herself, are deaf or living the restricted life of an invalid.

"Letter to the Deaf," originally a magazine article, was frequently reprinted as a booklet for deaf readers by charitable or cooperative agencies concerned with the welfare of the deaf. Despite its original issue to the general audience of *Tait's Edinburgh Magazine*, she makes it plain that she is addressing her article to deaf readers only and that she is unconcerned about the reactions "of those who do not belong to our fraternity."[31]

Throughout the essay she argues strongly in favor of the deaf achieving and maintaining as much autonomy as possible and regards the protectiveness of friends and relatives as harmful, "in as far as it encourages us to evade our enemy instead of grappling with it." Anything that prevents the deaf person from fully acknowledging and understanding the nature of his or her deafness is seen as inimical to the necessary demystification of the subject: "Advice must go for nothing with us in a case where nobody is qualified to advise. We must cross-question our physician, and hold him to it till he has told us all. We must destroy the sacredness of the subject, by speaking of it ourselves; not perpetually and sentimentally, but, when occasion arises, boldly, cheerfully, and as a plain matter of fact."[32] She suggests that the deaf inform strangers immediately of their disability in order to avoid confusion and mystery. At the same time she carefully points out that the deaf should not interfere with the ease of communication between those who hear adequately by asking for remarks to be repeated for their benefit.

She outlines the undesirable personality traits that are likely to arise from deafness:

the persuasion that people are taking advantage of us in what they say,—that they are discussing us, or laughing at us,—that they do not care for us as long as they are merry,—that the friend who takes the pains to talk to us might make us less conspicuous if he would,— the vehement desire that we might be let alone, and the sense of neglect if too long let alone; all these, absurd and wicked fancies as they are seen to be when fairly set down, have beset us all in our time; have they not?[33]

These distortions of perspective are best combatted, she suggests, by trying, in as far as the degree of deafness permits, to extend the diminished aural faculty by deliberately seeking out such sounds as are audible to the hard of hearing: the street barrel-organ, the rushing of a stream, or "the sough of words without the sense" of a House of Commons debate. She suggests, too, that the deaf combat their natural tendency to shun society and that they develop an active social life to avoid becoming "selfish, or absorbed in what does not concern our day and generation, or nervous, dependant, [sic] and helpless in common affairs."[34]

In *Life in the Sickroom* and "Letter to the Deaf," Martineau is primarily interested in the psychological rather than the physical effects of disability. Unlike the earlier article, *Life in the Sickroom* was published anonymously, though there can have been little doubt about its authorship. It, too, is addressed to those in similar situations rather than to a general audience, and she takes advantage of the more lengthy book format to devote ten pages to a dedication to "some fellow-sufferer" whom she hopes could benefit from such a book.

Typically, as well as giving advice on how to combat the oppressiveness of confinement to bed or to a single room, Martineau is eloquent about the ways in which the experience of invalidism can be turned into an opportunity for moral education. For example, she suggests that the restricted life of the sickroom dweller may give an opportunity to develop a more tolerant view of the world.

She constantly warns her readers against the dangers of invalid isolation leading to a distorted subjective view of the world, and to this end advises against the invalid's keeping a diary. She also writes at considerable length about the necessity of an invalid's having a view of the outside world from the sickroom. She writes vividly of the view from her own window, which shows her children flying their kites, lovers and friends walking together, the washerwomen with loads of laundry on their heads, "and the mistress of the garden, bringing up her pails of frothing milk from the cow-house, looks about her with complacency, and comes forth with fresh alacrity to cut the young lettuces which are sent for, for somebody's supper of cold lamb."[35]

Martineau's urging her readers, in both "Letter to the Deaf" and *Life in the Sickroom,* to set aside subjectivity and isolation in favor of observation of and participation in the social world echoes one of the most persistent themes of nineteenth-century writing. We find it expounded by Dickens in the broad strokes of *A Christmas Carol* (1843) when Scrooge is converted from miserliness to convivial sociability. George Eliot's exploration of the shift away from self-absorption to empathy with others is much subtler and more complex. She describes the process most eloquently in *Middlemarch* (1872) through the development of Dorothea Brooke from the totally self-absorbed girl who yearns after the life of a Saint Theresa to the woman who, at the end of the novel, watches the dawn workers from her window and feels herself "a part of that involuntary, palpitating life, and could neither look out on it from her luxurious shelter as a mere spectator, nor hide her eyes in a selfish complaining."[36] Martineau's description of invalid life and particularly her essay on the view from her sickroom window has much in common with George Eliot's description of Dorothea Brooke's shift in moral consciousness as she watches the scene from her window. As elsewhere in Victorian literature when this theme occurs, Martineau's exploration of it owes its force to the power of the conflicting impulses of the longing for seclusion and the profound desire to be involved in and to comprehend human society. The moral education which Martineau outlines for her "fellow-sufferers" in her essay for the deaf and in her book for invalids is a programmatic and prescriptive form of the conflict between the two powerful impulses which gives Victorian literature much of its energy and interest.

Chapter Four

Martineau as a Fiction Writer

Illustrations of Political Economy

The utilitarian philosophy which offered the "greatest happiness of the greatest number" as the ultimate social goal attempted to provide a remedy for all social ills through the doctrine of "political economy." Most notably, Adam Smith's *Inquiry Concerning the Wealth of Nations* (1776) provided an economic counterpart to the utilitarian theories of Jeremy Bentham by arguing for free trade and maximum freedom of economic competition as the economic means by which the greatest happiness of the greatest number could be achieved. Although Smith greatly influenced the formative ideas of philosophers like John Stuart Mill and middle-class intellectuals like Martineau, the "principles of political economy," widely thought of by utilitarian adherents as a "science," were largely unknown beyond the middle class.

By the time Martineau began the first numbers of her *Illustrations of Political Economy* (1832–34) there had already been two attempts to popularize the theories. Mrs. Marcet's *Conversations on Political Economy* (1816) and James Mill the Elder's *Elements of Political Economy* (1812) had both been aimed primarily at an audience of young readers. Martineau's object was to reach working-class readers, anticipating the time when they would be fully enfranchised.

The format of the series was of self-contained monthly numbers, individual volumes, each one no longer than a long short story. Each number described a particular social problem and then applied a solution in accordance with the theory of political economy. Thus *Demerara* dealt with slavery, *A Manchester Strike* with labor unrest, *Weal and Woe in Garveloch* with population increase, and so on. Each topic was painstakingly researched, especially through government blue books, the official reports that were beginning to chart the social and economic problems of the time. Despite Martineau's attempt to digest complex information of this kind, the tales inevitably strike the modern readers as simplistic and somewhat preachy. Occasionally, however, there are glimpses of a genuine imaginative gift, as in *A Manchester Strike*, which prefigures the more complex and satisfying portraits of industrial life in Dickens's *Hard Times* (1854) or Mrs. Gaskell's *North and South* (1855).

The two series that she produced to follow *Illustrations of Political Economy* offer no such relief from dry didacticism. *Illustrations of Taxation* (1834) attempted to show the need for taxation reform. For example, in *The Tenth Haycock* she attacked the practice of tithing for the established church and in *The Scholars of Arneside* she examined the effects of the stamp tax on newspapers, making a surprisingly harsh attack on the radical working-class press. Her *Forest and Game Law Tales* (1845) and *Dawn Island* (1845) were written on behalf of the Anti-Corn Law League to promote their arguments against protectionist trade legislation. Martineau's contemporaries were moved by these accounts of the hardships endured by country dwellers, especially those resulting from the heavy legal penalties for poaching, but as fiction they are insufficiently realized to be read today as much more than economic homilies.

Vera Wheatley comments that in the *Illustrations of Political Economy* "is to be found the novelist manqué, the novelist impaired, even blasted by the passionate urge for propaganda and reform."[1] Her remark reflects a typical response of most modern readers to Martineau's illustrative and didactic tales: the explicitness of the "principles" that are pointed out in the course of the narrative and then summarized at the end of each volume strikes the modern reader as both naive and heavy-handed. We wonder at the appetite for "morals" of Martineau's nineteenth-century readers, especially when we arrive at the final volume of the political economy tales to find that the last "tale," *The Morals of Many Fables*, is simply a collection of the "principles" which have appeared at the end of each preceding volume. It is impossible now to reconstruct a full sense of the readership that received the *Illustrations of Political Economy* and later didactic fables with such enthusiasm. One clue lies in the sheer novelty of simple educative literature directed at an audience of adult readers many of whom were newly literate. A review from a newspaper published in Martineau's home town of Norwich gives an indication of the readership of the tales: "We call upon all those who love their country, who would wish to see their fellow-countrymen happy, contented, wealthy, and wise, to disseminate as widely as it is possible, not only among those who can read, but even among those who have not yet enjoyed the good effects of the schoolmaster, in order that they may hear read, this cheap and unpretending little volume, which, while it teaches how to spread around the greatest good to the greatest number, inculcates a morality which must lead to the best results."[2] Many readers who had "not yet enjoyed the good effects of the schoolmaster" undoubtedly did enjoy Martineau's tales, not least because her didacticism is unusually open and straightforward, shot through with naive enthusiasm rather than high-handed sermonizing. Other working-class readers were almost certainly skeptical about the "principles" of political economy that Martineau asserted so uncritically in the series: "The juggle of the political economists . . . is now seen through; when translated into plain English, political economy means nothing more or less than this—Give up the whole produce of your labour—fill everybody's cupboard but your own—and then starve quietly!!!"[3]

Whether or not they agreed with Martineau's views, her contemporary readers would certainly have regarded the subjects covered in the political economy series as urgently topical. Martineau herself was evidently stimulated by a sense of actively participating in the important events of the day when writing a tale on a subject that was a current topic of parliamentary debate: "I sat down to read it [the new Poor Law Bill] with no little emotion, and some apprehension; and the moment when, arriving at the end, I found that the government scheme and my own were identical, point by point, was not one to be easily forgotten. I never wrote anything with more glee than 'The Hamlets,'—the number in which the proposed reform is exemplified: and the spirit of the work carried me through the great effort of writing that number and 'Cinnamon and Pearls' in one month,—during a country visit in glorious summer weather" (1:221–22).

Like Dickens and Mrs. Gaskell, Martineau is much preoccupied with the subject of unions, factory legislation, and strikes. Her doctrinaire theories of political economy lead her to argue obduratedly that the interests of worker and capital are identical despite all the evidence to the contrary. In many ways the fictional portrait of workers and their unions she presents is very similar to that presented by Mrs. Gaskell in *North and South* or by Dickens in *Hard Times*. All three make a distinction between the "responsible" working men like Martineau's William Allen or Dickens's Stephen Blackpool in *Hard Times* and the rabble-rousing orator who stirs such men to political action against their own best interests. The scenario was a comforting one to middle-class readers. All efforts of workers to improve their conditions of employment could then be seen as the interference of the mysterious figures usually referred to, in a twentieth-century context, as "outside agitators." Both Dickens and Mrs. Gaskell, however, take the grievances of workers a good deal more seriously than Martineau, who argues relentlessly against legislation establishing proper wages as an infringement of the workers' freedom to sell their labor in a "free" market: "wages-laws involve the same absurdity as the combination laws we are so glad to have got rid of. Every man who is not a slave has the right to ask a price for his labor. . . ."[4]

Even within the cramped confines of Martineau's dogmatic laissez-faire views, there is a glimpse of a considerable fictional power in the way in which, for example, she sketches the figure of William Allen at the end of *The Manchester Strike* as a totally demoralized and alienated figure as a result of his unsuccessful attempt to lead a strike. Yet here, as well as in her tale about machine-breaking, *The Turn Out,* her perspective on her working characters is always essentially that of the bombazine manufacturer's daughter rather than of an observer who fully grasps the significance of the ferment of industrial unrest in the textile factories.

Demerara, which had the effect of making Martineau notorious among antiabolitionists in America, is, for all its undisguised didactic intentions, a surprisingly well-realized work of fiction. Although much of it is thoroughly contrived, it has some powerful moments, particularly when Martineau steps beyond the strictly economic argument and reveals the climate of covert fear and loathing that existed between slave and owner. The long commination against his master offered up by one of the slaves as his only prayer in the chapter understatedly headed

"Christianity Difficult in Demerara" is powerful and convincing. More subtly, Martineau reveals the disparity between slave owners' avowals that the relationship between master and slave is one of benign protective custody and the underlying terror of all slave owners that they and their families may become the victims of violent slave mutiny: "The cause of all this terror now flashed upon Alfred: the same cause which made Mitchelson carry his family with him wherever he went. He was afraid to leave his household in the power of his slaves. Yet this was the country where (so people are told in England) slaves are contented and happy, and, in every respect, better off than the free peasantry of the empire."[5] Similarly, the scene in which the slaves "accidentally" botch the rescue of the overseer Horner from the flood so that he is drowned in a rushing torrent to the accompanying cheers of his apparent rescuers gives the reader an insight into the moral vortex of a slave-owning society infinitely more eloquent than the sentimental appeal made in *Uncle Tom's Cabin* (1852) a few decades later.

The social ideals that Martineau promotes in the *Illustrations of Political Economy* and in her other didactic works are best summarized in the picture of idyllic well-ordered village life she provides at the end of *Brooke and Brooke Farm,* which is characterized by indefatigable labor and shrewd planning and management based strictly on the principles of political economy:

George was a pattern of industry. Before and after his hours of daily labor, he was seen digging, hoeing, planting, and pruning in his garden; his boys and sometimes his wife helping him; his eldest girl tending the cow, and the others mending or knitting stockings, or cleaning the house. Even the very little ones earned many a shilling by cutting a particular sort of grass in the lanes for seed for Mr. Malton's pasture land. Each with a pair of scissors, they cut the tops off about six inches long, and filled their sack in a few hours. Mr. Malton's steward paid them threepence a bushel for it, measured as hay. Their work was made easier by this grass being sown in lines along the hedges; and it was well worth the little trouble this cost to secure a constant supply of the seed which was greatly in request; the sheep being very fond of this pasture.

Gray's boys had all shoes and stockings now, and the girls were tidily dressed. The rent was regularly paid, and their fare was improved. How happened this?—From having ground and keeping a cow?—Not entirely, though in some measure. The wages of labor had risen considerably at Brooke since the common was inclosed, as there was more work to be done, and the number of hands had not increased in proportion, though the population was already one-third larger than five years before. Gray felt the advantage of this rise of wages, and of having his family employed. He now wondered at his neighbors for letting their children be wholly idle as much as we once wondered at him.[6]

Significantly, the crowning feature of this picture of orderly management and prosperity is the schoolhouse. Over and over again in Martineau's work we find her returning to the theme that education rather than legislation will eventually prove the more effective means of improving the lives of working people. This conviction that social progress was the result of changes in attitude derived from education underlies the sense of a crusading mission in the tales. Undoubtedly Martineau believed that her tales would educate her audience to the principles of political economy and that this would be the most effective means of bringing about important social changes. It should also be noted that among nineteenth-century writers it is most frequently the women writers who perceive education in itself as a form of salvation. Although in an age in which the idea of formal education as a universal right was gradually gaining ground, the idea of education as a panacea was a fairly common one, it is noticeable that the women writers are most apt to fix on the idea with real passion. Instances abound in the works of novelists like Charlotte Brontë, Elizabeth Gaskell, and George Eliot in which education is shown to have a beneficent effect on the lives of the characters, but Martineau's tales and her expository writing contain some of the most ardent pleas for the value of education. Indeed, unlike such writers as Charlotte Brontë, Martineau's writings scarcely admit that such a thing as a bad school can exist. For her, the schoolhouse, like the one at the end of *Brooke and Brooke Farm,* is almost invariably presented as an unequivocal symbol of social progress.

Novels: *The Hour and the Man* and *Deerbrook*

Martineau wrote only two full-length works of fiction intended for adult readers. *The Hour and the Man* (1841) is by far the less successful of the two. In it Martineau attempts to set the historical record straight concerning the character and the career of the Haitian popular leader Toussaint L'Ouverture, who had died in a French prison at the end of the previous century after leading a rebellion against French colonial rule. Toussaint had been vilified in French accounts of his capture and death and, perhaps, because of this, had become something of a minor popular hero to the British. He had been the subject of a sonnet by Wordsworth, "Toussaint the most unhappy Man of Men!"[7] Martineau, however, had first become interested in Toussaint's career through reading an article in the *Quarterly Review* on the history of Haiti. She reacted with immediate enthusiasm and wrote in her diary: "it flashed across me that my novel must be on the Haytian [*sic*] revolution, and Toussaint my hero. Was ever any subject more splendid, more fit than this for me and my purposes? One generally knows when the right idea, the true inspiration, comes, and I have a strong persuasion that this will prove my first great work of fiction. It admits of romance, it furnishes me with a story, it will do a world of good to the slave question, it is heroic in its character, and it leaves me English domestic life for a change Hereafter" (3:216). Some of Martineau's criteria offered here in her recognition of the "right idea" give us some significant clues to her approach to the novel. She is noticeably grateful for a ready-made story and, even more importantly, sees the resulting novel as doing "a world of good" in the struggle against slavery.

She proposed the idea of a novel based on Toussaint's career to a friend but received such a discouraging response that she set the plan aside. She had continued, however, to be sufficiently intrigued by the subject during her 1838 travels in Europe to go out of her way to see the prison at Joux in which Toussaint had died and to visit his nearby grave. Two years later, when confined to her Tynemouth sickroom, she returned to her original idea.

Martineau's difficulties with fictional structure are more evident in *The Hour and the Man* than anywhere else in her work. The narrative sequence is often extremely difficult to follow because new characters are introduced and then abandoned. The majority of these structural difficulties arise from Martineau's decision to write a fictional biography rather than an historical account. She seems to have felt compelled to dramatize

every known event of Toussaint's life to the fullest possible
extent. As a result, there is no building of pace and tension,
but rather the reader has the impression of a flat gallop from
beginning to end.

Martineau used the term "novel" for only one of her fictional
works. *Deerbrook* (1842) is based on the story which Martineau
had heard of a family friend who "had been cruelly driven,
by a match-making lady, to propose to the sister of the woman
he loved,—on private information that the elder had lost her
heart to him, and that he had shown her attention enough to
warrant it. The marriage was not a very happy one, good as
were the persons concerned, in their various ways. I altered
the circumstances as much as I could, and drew the character,
not of our English but of an American friend, whose domestic
position is altogether different . . ." (2:113). The theme of
three lives blighted by a mistaken marriage choice based on
social pressure is one that would have fully taxed the gifts of
either a George Eliot or a Henry James. Although the emotional
hothouse atmosphere of resentment and sexual jealousy that
exists between the young doctor, Hope, and the two sisters,
Hester and Margaret, was evidently beyond Martineau's powers
as a novelist, her account of the way in which the three come
to terms with the constraints of their lives is a surprisingly convincing one. Martineau's hero is a man condemned to inhabit
the nightmare of having married the "wrong" sister. He is still
in love with Margaret Ibbotson, who, after the custom of the
day, was to live with the newly married couple as a companion
for her sister: "A strange trouble—a fearful suspicion had seized
upon him. He was amazed at the return of his feelings about
Margaret, and filled with horror when he thought of the days,
and months, and years of close domestic companionship with
her, from which there was no escape. There was no escape.
The peace of his wife, of Margaret—his own peace in theirs—
depended wholly on the deep secrecy in which he should pre-
serve the mistake he had made. It was a mistake. He could
scarcely endure the thought; but it was so" (*D,* 176).

However, the most intense emotional dynamic in the novel
is the relationship between the two sisters. Martineau's portrait
of the way in which Hester possessively interferes with her
sister's pursuits and friendships, insisting that she herself must

be her only close companion, is particularly well-observed. Especially convincing is the way in which the possessive Hester nourishes a deep sense of personal grievance. She accuses her sister: "You go to others for the comfort your ought to seek in me. You place that confidence in others which ought to be mine alone. You are cheered when you learn that the commonest gossips in Deerbrook care about you, and you set no value on your own sister's feelings for you. You have faith and charity for people out of doors, and mistrust and misconstruction for those at home. I am the injured one, Margaret, not you" (*D*, 248). Even though the emotional conflict of the scene is truthfully rendered, Martineau seems to feel compelled to replace the real drama of the struggle between the sisters with an absurdly melodramatic conclusion: "She raised herself up on the sofa, and timidly held out her hand to her sister. Hester thrust it away. Margaret uttered a cry of agony, such as had never been heard from her since her childhood. Hope fell on the floor—he had fainted at the sound" (*D*, 248). The scene is strikingly reminiscent of the domestic melodrama which was to become so popular on the stage later on in the century. Probably, however, what we are seeing here is not so much an identifiable theatrical influence as a simple failing to sustain a dramatic fictional scene within its own terms and based on its own internal logic. Quite simply, the most powerful dynamic element in the scene is the conflict between the two sisters, and Martineau seems uncertain as to what Hope's role and his response should be. Unable to find a better way of removing a problematical and extraneous character from the action, she simply has him lose consciousness in a faint.

Florid overwriting of this kind is usually the result of a lack of confidence on the part of the writer and is generally based on a sense of uncertainty about the dramatic effect already achieved. In this respect Martineau's modest estimate of her own fictional abilities becomes a kind of self-fulfilling prophecy whereby the power of her writing is undermined by her insecurity about her capabilities.

Deerbrook is strongest when Martineau portrays the petty conflicts that make up the fabric of village life rather than where she attempts to deal with the major emotional drama of love and jealousy. Of all Martineau's fiction, *Deerbrook* is the most

strongly rooted in a sense of place. Much of the scenery is
based on her memories of the country house of a relative to
whom she was sent for the sake of her health when she was
eight years old. One of the main strengths of *Deerbrook* as a
novel is Martineau's acute sense of the ironic contrast between
the idyllic appearance of the village and its spacious houses
and the cramped and constrained lives resulting from village
hypocrisies and conventions. The fantasy of a peaceful country
life is the starting point for the novel:

> Every town-bred person who travels in a rich country region, knows
> what it is to see a neat white house planted in a pretty situation,—
> in a shrubbery, or commanding a sunny common, or nestling between
> two hills,—and to say to himself, as the carriage sweeps past its gate,
> "I should like to live there,"—"I could be very happy in that pretty
> place." Transient visions pass before his mind's-eye of dewy summer
> mornings, when the shadows are long on the grass, and of bright
> autumn afternoons, when it would be luxury to saunter in the neigh-
> bouring lanes; and of frosty winter days, when the sun shines in over
> the laurustinus at the window, while the fire burns with a different
> light from that which it gives in the dull parlours of the city. (*D,* 1)

The town-bred Hester and Margaret Ibbotson arrive in Deerbrook with precisely this sense of optimism about country life
but quickly find that village protocol is infinitely more restrictive
than anything they have known in Birmingham. They plan to
go for a walk together but Sophia Grey runs after them with
a message from her mother: "mamma wished they would be
so good as to defer their walk; mamma was afraid that if they
were seen abroad in the village, it would be supposed that they
did not wish to receive visitors: mamma would rather that they
should stay within this morning. There was nothing for it but
to turn back; and Hester threw down her bonnet with no very
good grace, as she observed to her sister that, to all appearance,
a town life was more free than a country one, after all" (*D,*
24).

Mrs. Grey, who interferes so disastrously in Hope's courtship,
is one of the most complex minor characters. The subtlety of
Martineau's portrait of a woman who pries and interferes with
others' lives not so much out of malice but because her own
life is unexciting would not be out of place in a Jane Austen

novel. The way in which the difficulties of other people's lives present such a person with a relief from the monotony of her own is subtlely sketched in Mrs. Grey's response to the series of disasters that overtakes Hope: "Mrs. Grey's countenance wore an expression of solemn misery with a little of the complacency of excitement about it" (*D*, 237).

Like other nineteenth-century novelists, Martineau tends to see economic and social factors as playing a very significant role in the development of her characters' attitudes. Throughout the novel she makes it clear that Mrs. Grey is as she is mainly because village life leaves little room for anything but petty conniving for a woman of her social class and position.

One of the most interesting analyses of character arising from social circumstance in *Deerbrook* is the portrait of the governess, Maria Young. Unlike Anne Brontë in *Agnes Gray*, Martineau does not explore the pattern of humiliation which arises from the relationship between the governess and the family that employs her but dwells rather on the solitariness of the occupation, the frustrations and the limitations of teaching only a narrow range of knowledge, the long hours of work, and the penurious wages. Maria Young counsels stoicism as the only possible recourse in her situation: "let a governess learn what to expect; set her free from hankering after happiness in her work and you have a happy governess!" (*D*, 21). A similarly bleak stoicism is presented as the best means of Hope tolerating his marriage: "Let us put the thought of making happiness out of our minds altogether. . . . I am persuaded that half the misery in the world comes from straining after happiness!" (*D*, 145).

Despite her loneliness, Maria Young's lot is seen as in some ways preferable to that of Hester and Margaret. She, at least, has work to do while the more leisured life of the sisters presents the prospect of frittering away their days in futile or trivial occupations. Events intervene to save Hope and his wife and sister-in-law from a life of comfortable ennui. Hope votes against the candidate supported by the local landowner in the election and the whole family is shunned by the community. His medical practice collapses under the pressure of malicious rumors and they are forced to undertake their own household manual work for the first time in their lives. Physical work has the immediate effect of freeing them from the pettiness and emotional claustrophobia that has blighted their domestic life. Their existence is, quite suddenly, pleasurable and meaningful: "The three who sat down to breakfast were as reasonable and philosophical as most people; but even they were taken by surprise with the sweetness of comforts provided by their own immediate toil. There was something in the novelty, perhaps; but Hope threw on the fire with remarkable energy the coals he had himself brought in from the coal-house, and ate with great relish the toast toasted by his wife's own hands. Margaret, too, looked round the room more than once with a new sort of pride in there not being a particle of dust on table, chair or book" (*D,* 465).

At first sight this preoccupation might seem the product of a Puritan inclination whereby the virtues of hard work are extolled as part of a general asceticism. In fact, she is often eloquent about the effects of grinding or routine work. Maria Young speaks feelingly in *Deerbrook* about the often futile and exhausting work of being a governess and explains how much more intensely she experiences her rare moments of leisure: "Let none pretend to understand the value of such whose lives are all leisure; who take up a book to pass the time; who saunter in gardens because there are no morning visits to make; who exaggerate the writing of a family letter into important business. Such have their own enjoyments: but they know nothing of the paroxysm of pleasure of a really hardworking person on hearing the door shut which excludes the business of life . . ." (*D,* 32–33). Martineau makes a clear distinction between the type of work to which those like Maria are condemned day in and day out by relentless necessity and, on the other hand, the salutary experience of the previously privileged who are suddenly compelled to make contact with mundane realities like shoveling snow or preparing food, tasks from which they had previously been cushioned by their economic and social status. In some respects, though, she sees hard work, whether for Maria Young or for Edward Hope and his family, rather as Chekov does in *Uncle Vanya,* as a solution to lives which have been otherwise blighted through unwise choices or through external constraints.

Martineau caters to her readers' tastes by providing a less austere conclusion than that of salvation through hard work alone. Hope inherits a small bequest and is able to resume his medical practice. Margaret marries the relatively wealthy Philip Enderby and thus, at the end of the novel, economic prosperity is restored to all three central characters. Yet the abiding impression throughout is that the severest difficulties can best be ameliorated, not by marrying well or inheriting a fortune, but by hard work. "Come, let us be up and doing" (*D,* 208), says Margaret, when the whole family is being shunned and pilloried by the villagers. Her admonition expresses the resolve in adversity that Martineau most admires, and the reader has the distinct impression that the fortuitous wealth which the characters receive at the end of the novel is essentially a reward for their grace in adversity.

Although Martineau's portrait of the corrosive petty rivalries of a small community in *Deerbrook* begins in a quiet *Cranford*-life atmosphere, it incorporates a *grand guignol* tone as the narrative progresses. Once Hope has voted against the favored candidate in the election, his medical practice is ruined by the spreading of rumours about body-snatching and accidental poisoning of patients. Hester goes to the husband of the woman who has instigated most of the rumors and demands a public retraction: "I would have you see that every false charge she has brought is retracted—every vile insinuation recanted. You must make her say everywhere that my husband has no stolen dead bodies; that he is not a plotter against the peace and order of society; that he has not poisoned a child by mistake, or cut off a sound limb for sake of practice and amusement. Your wife has said these things, and you know it; and you must make her contradict them all" (*D,* 307).

Martineau's documentation of the way in which political unpopularity can escalate to hysterical rumor-spreading and even mob violence is undoubtedly a perceptive and accurate account of the partisan politics of the day. Yet she frequently seems to lack confidence in her ability to dramatize the events themselves and resorts instead to melodrama in such episodes as the theft and restoration of a ring or in the way in which her characters accompany the dialogue with stagy gestures and exclamations. It may be that this reliance on crude melodramatic effects arose partly from an uncertainty of intention. On the one hand, Martineau admired Jane Austen and deliberately attempted to emulate

her manner of portraying provincial life. She noted in her diary
that *Emma* was "most admirable," but also that "The complexities of the story are beyond my comprehension, and wonderfully
beautiful" (3:218). For all her admiration of Austen, one senses
that Martineau was apt in her own writing to become impatient
with the "little complexities" and the miniscule dramas of provincial life and to yearn after a wider canvas which could show
such events in their broader political context. Consequently,
she often attempts to evoke a response from the reader by means
of a melodramatic short cut rather than, like Jane Austen, patiently showing each scene evolving with its own inevitable logic.

Deerbrook is a seriously flawed novel, but it is one that remains
worth reading for the modern student of nineteenth-century
literature if only for the insight it provides on social and political
life. Her account of partisan politics and corruption in an election, for example, is one of the most detailed and revealing
to be found in a nineteenth-century novel. The novel as a whole
remains frustrating reading, however, for the glimpses it gives
us of a powerful but unevenly developed fictional gift.

The Playfellow

Martineau's four children's stories first published in a single
volume under the title *The Playfellow* (1841) remain her only
works that have continued to be regularly republished for a
general audience. Although *Feats on the Fiord* has proved the
most popular of the four, in that it has been more frequently
reprinted, it is far less successful than *The Crofton Boys* over
which George Eliot had such "delightful crying."[20] *Feats on the
Fiord* frequently appears as the solitary mention of Martineau's
work in histories of children's literature, while (with the notable
exception of Kathleen Tillotson in *The Novels of the Eighteen
Forties*)[9] *The Crofton Boys* is very rarely discussed by critics or
literary historians. All four stories, however, remain eminently
readable and certainly rank as Martineau's most successful efforts
in fiction.

The central idea of *The Settlers at Home* arose from Martineau's
reading an article by De Quincey about snowstorms. She toyed
with the idea of writing a story in which a snowstorm was the
major event but decided that a flood was a less hackneyed natural

disaster in fiction. She studied Thomas Dick Lauder's book about the 1829 floods in Morayshire and articles about the Lincolnshire fenland in Knight's *Penny Cyclopadia.* The character of Roger Redfurn was gleaned largely from an account of a Gypsy she had read in one of the Poor Law Reports.

Compared with some of the *Illustrations of Political Economy,* where the source material seems to have been hastily patched together into a narrative, *The Settlers at Home* has a relatively seamless construction. Her story relies, like so many children's books, on the situation in which children are separated from their parents or guardians and forced to survive as best they can. Countless children's books rely on this device of temporary or permanent orphanhood of the child characters to bring about a Robinson Crusoe–like situation in which the children pit their wits against an unfriendly or an unfamiliar environment. Captain Marryat used this formula in his children's adventure tales like *Masterman Ready* (1841), *Settlers in Canada* (1844), and *Children of the New Forest* (1847). In the 1850s R. M. Ballantyne's boys' stories interwove the Crusoe formula with an empire-building theme intended to stir patriotic fervour. The same formula has continued to be popular among twentieth-century writers for children, though they are apt to release their parentless child characters into less threatening environments.

The children in *The Settlers at Home* lose their parents in a flood and have to feed and shelter themselves, a servant, and their baby brother with the grudging and intermittent help of the Gypsy boy, Roger Redfurn. Martineau does not flinch from portraying the real dangers of the flood for her child readers. People and animals are drowned, houses destroyed, and the children's baby brother dies when they can no longer obtain milk for him because their cow has starved to death. The flood itself has been the result, not of strictly natural causes, but of the malice of neighboring townspeople toward the settlers of French and Dutch origin who had fled to England because of religious persecution. The bleak picture is relieved somewhat at the end of the story when the children are rescued and there is some suggestion that Roger the Gypsy is likely to undergo a gradual moral reform, but no assurance is given that the townspeople's xenophobia, which caused the deliberate flooding of the fenland, has really diminished.

Like the other three volumes of *The Playfellow*, *The Settlers at Home* is surprisingly free of either the didactic intention or the mawkish sentimentality that was the hallmark of the children's fiction of the period. It is surprising to realize that it was written at a time when, with a few notable exceptions like Catherine Sinclair's *Holiday House* (1813), there was very little fiction for children that was not crushingly didactic in the manner of Mrs. Sherwood's grim work, *The History of the Fairchild Family: or, The Child's Manual; being a collection of stories calculated to show the importance and effects of a Religious Education* (1818), with its notoriously gruesome scene in which the father lectures the children on the evils of theft under a gibbet carrying the decaying body of an executed felon. By no means all works intended for children were as unremittingly grim as Mrs. Sherwood's work, however. The boys' adventure stories which began to appear during the 1840s were relatively free of obvious didacticism, but the literature for children with a domestic rather than an exotic setting still tended to be self-conscious about its moral responsibilities to its audience.

In some respects it is rather surprising that Martineau should have chosen to write for children at all. During the 1840s children's literature barely existed either as a literary genre or as a commercial product. For the most part children were reading a selection of the literature intended for their elders. We can perhaps trace part of Martineau's impulse to write for children to the intensity of her own reading experiences as a child. As noted earlier, she could well recall in adult life the way in which her childhood imagination had been deeply stirred by reading Milton, and it may be that she was attracted by the idea of reaching an audience who might be similarly receptive.

Martineau believed *The Peasant and the Prince* to be the least popular of her *Playfellow* tales among child readers, though she does not speculate about the reasons for this. The most obvious hindrance to its popularity with children is the fact that, unlike the other three *Playfellow* tales, all its principal characters were adults. Interestingly enough, however, she remarks in her *Autobiography* that *The Peasant and the Prince* was extremely popular "among poor people, who read it with wonderful eagerness. Some of them called it 'the French revelation,' and the copy in Lending Libraries was more thumbed than the others"

(2:161). The book is less a work of fiction than an absorbing simplified historical account of the final days of the French monarchy during the revolution. We see Martineau as a popular historian at her best, showing how the protected, blinkered lives of the monarchy made them unable to understand either the people's genuine grievances or the force of the wave of powerful popular feeling which had resulted from centuries of oppression.

The structure of the story as an intended work of fiction presents serious problems. She devotes the first four chapters to a mini-narrative of peasant hardship, but focuses the rest of the book on the fate of the monarchy. The title is therefore a misleading one, since it leads the reader to expect some fictional link between the fate of the peasants and that of the royal characters. In fact, the only link is the episode in which the carriage of the young Marie Antoinette passes through the village when she is on her way to be married to Louis XVI. Martineau's story is plagued by the same fictional dilemma as troubled Dickens in *A Tale of Two Cities.* Both writers wish to stress the real oppression experienced by peasants and by the poor in cities, but the description of scenes of mob violence by their very nature swing the reader's sympathies toward the beleaguered aristocrats and monarchy who, within the framework of the story, begin to seem like the real victims.

Despite the intrinsic difficulties presented by the subject itself and despite the further problems created by the divided narrative, Martineau's account of the last days of the French royal family sustains a dramatic tension throughout. She ends the work with a brief appeal to her readers to recognize that "It is not only France that has been ignorant, and guilty, and miserable. Every country is full of blessings given by the hand of God; and in every country are those blessings misused, more or less, as they were in France."[10] The events of the French Revolution were by no means remote to the early Victorian sensibility, and Martineau's brief account is one of the most balanced of those to be addressed to a popular audience. However even-handed Martineau's treatment of the Revolution may seem to the modern reader, the subject at the time was a sufficiently inflammatory one for her old enemy the *Quarterly Review* to condemn *The Peasant and the Prince* out of hand as a work "which has a reprehensible purpose and tendency."[11]

Feats on the Fiord is now Martineau's single best-known work. The reasons for its continued popularity are fairly evident. By luck or good judgment she hit upon a plot which built and sustained tension and interest. Although at times the Norwegian setting is rather contrived, and some descriptions of scenery and customs give the impression of having been written with guide book or encyclopedia in hand, the narrative is an extremely absorbing one. The story interweaves two central ideas. Throughout, especially with the character of the housemaid, Erica, Martineau stresses the "superstitious" beliefs of the Norwegian peasantry in malicious evil spirits like Nipen, the wood demon. The real threat to the security of their community, however, is from the pirates who rob and loot isolated farm houses and villages. Rolf, Erica's betrothed, who does not believe in wood demons and water spirits, is able to manipulate the pirates' own superstitious fear of these spirits to bring about their defeat and capture. Even though belief in wood and water spirits is shown throughout the novel as primitive and irrational, Martineau succeeds in avoiding a patronizing tone by presenting Kollsen, the pastor, who argues sententiously and relentlessly against "superstition" as being almost comically pompous and insensitive.

The story has many of the ingredients of an exciting adventure tale: chase, escape, a secret hiding place, disguise, and a final battle in which the pirates are ambushed when attempting to loot a farmstead. It has more depth, however, than the fast-moving action tales involving similar elements which later writers like Marryat and Ballantyne were to develop. Many of the figures are constructed from something more than the pasteboard which one usually expects in adventure stories. For example, Hund, the villain who betrays the villagers, is a relatively complex figure, not so much conventionally wicked as doomed and haunted by his evil deed in the past when he saved himself from the wolves by sacrificing two small children in his stead. Despite the restrictions on character development within the framework of an adventure tale, we see Erica, one of the two central figures in the story, gradually shed her pantheon of wood and water spirits and grope toward a more rational sense of cause and effect in the world. Throughout *Feats on the Fiord* there is a surprising sureness of touch which makes the tale an outstanding example of early Victorian fiction for children.

By far the most sensitive and complex work in *The Playfellow* is *The Crofton Boys,* which has the distinction of being the first work written for children in English which fully merits the genre-description of "psychological novel." It tells the story of Hugh Procter, the youngest son of a chemist and druggist who lives in central London. Hugh longs to attend Crofton School where his older brother Phil is a pupil. Fed by his brother's stories of life at school, his only ideal is to be a "Crofton Boy." Though he is really too young to be enrolled at boarding school his parents relent since they feel he is already too abstracted by his fantasies of Crofton to pursue his home studies with the governess with much success. Once enrolled at the school, Hugh discovers that his youth and his dreamy abstracted personality present difficulties with his studies and with dealing with the rigid ethos of a public school. His troubles at school are brought to a sudden crisis by an accident in which he is pulled from the top of a wall by a group of his classmates, and his foot is crushed by a heavy coping stone that has been loosened by the frost. His crushed foot has to be amputated, and the remainder of the story is concerned with how Hugh adjusts to his disability and attempts to reintegrate himself into the life of the school. Hugh matures largely as a result of adjusting to his lameness and through his friendship with Holt who at first displays some of the babyishness and self-indulgence which Hugh himself has had to outgrow. Hugh's puzzle over his future is resolved when Holt's father offers to have the two boys educated together and to secure Hugh a position in the Indian Civil Service. This plan salvages Hugh's dream of travel, which he had earlier feared would be precluded by his lameness.

Martineau's portrait of Hugh Procter is one of the subtlest explorations of a child's state of mind in nineteenth-century children's books. His straining to emulate the behavior of his older brother and his fantasies about school life are sketched with striking insight and sensitivity. She captures perfectly the excited, preoccupied mental state of a child going to school for the first time:

The sun seemed to Hugh to glare very much; and he thought he had never known the streets so noisy, or the people so pushing. The

truth was, his heart was beating so he could hardly see: and yet he
was so busy looking about him for a sight of the river, and everything
he wished to bid good-bye to, that his father, who held him fast by
the hand, shook him more than once, and told him he would run
everybody down if he could,—to judge by his way of walking.[12]

Hugh's ingenuousness proves a constant hazard in the context
of school life from the time when on his way to Crofton he is
excessively garrulous to the school usher about his "secret"
pocket for his money to his attempts to elicit compliments from
his schoolmates about a theme he has written. Martineau's point
of view in describing Hugh's experiences in such episodes is
very different from that of Thomas Hughes's *Tom Brown's School-
days* (1857) and the host of imitations that followed it. Hughes
tends to show the public school ethos in a relatively favorable
light and suggests that the brutality of characters like Flashman
and his friends is really an exception to the ethos rather than
a product of it. While Martineau's account does not make a
point of condemning the collective schoolboy attitudes that taboo "telling tales" under any circumstances or routinely mock
any boy with an unusual-sounding name, she sees these as part
of the taboo on the expression of tender feelings that pervades
schoolboy culture. Another boy gives Hugh an informal lecture
on what is expected of him in the chapter headed "What Is
Only To Be Had At Home":

"Ah! you don't understand school and schoolboys yet," replied Firth.
"To do a difficult lesson well is a grand affair at home, and the whole
house knows of it. But it is the commonest thing in the world here.
If you learn to feel with these boys, instead of expecting them to
feel with you (which they cannot possibly do), you will soon find
that they care for you accordingly."
   Hugh shook his head.
   "You will find it in every school in England," continued Firth,
"that it is not the way of boys to talk about feelings—about anybody's
feelings. That is the reason why they do not mention their sisters or
their mothers—except when two confidential friends are together,
in a tree, or by themselves in the meadows. But, as sure as ever a
boy is full of action—if he tops the rest at play—holds his tongue,
or helps others generously—or shows a manly spirit without being
proud of it, the whole school is his friend. You have done well, so

far, by growing more and more sociable; but you will lose ground if you boast about your lessons out of school. To prosper at Crofton, you must put off home, and make yourself a Crofton boy."[13]

Hugh "grows up," not by accepting the schoolboy ethos wholesale like Tom Brown, but as a result of his accident and the way in which he has to learn to cope with his disability. He takes his mother's advice that the wisest course is not to attempt to minimize the likely effects of his lameness, but rather to face all the hindrances coolly. One of his hardest lessons on his return to school is that, after the initial novelty, he is no longer the recipient of special treatment. He leaves his theme behind at his aunt and uncle's house and pleads for his brother or one of his companions to go and fetch it for him. Their early reluctance is followed by a rush of guilty volunteering when Hugh bursts into tears of frustration. A few moments later Hugh is clearly feeling guilty about his own selfishness: "Before Phil returned, it struck Hugh that he had been very selfish; and that it was not a good way of bearing his trial to impose on any one a walk of four miles, to repair a piece of carelessness of his own. Nobody blamed him; but he did not like to look in the faces round him to see what people thought."[14] The sensitivity of Martineau's dramatization of scenes like this almost certainly springs from her own lifelong awareness of the possibility of unlikeable character traits developing as a result of a disability. Her stern handling of the problems of her own deafness clearly gave her an insight into Hugh's striving to prevent his personality from becoming distorted through depending unnecessarily on others or "to make use of his privation to obtain indulgences for himself."[15]

The space devoted to analyzing Hugh's response to his disability is likely to seem disproportionate to most modern readers. John Rowe Townsend, for example, dismisses *The Crofton Boys* as "a somewhat harrowing didactic work whose hero is crippled for life at an early stage in the proceedings."[16] Townsend evidently finds the hearty muscular Christianity of the later boys' school stories more appealing, but his comment essentially misses the point. *The Crofton Boys*, while it has two or three explicit didactic passages, is not nearly as committed to promoting a particular ideology as the better-known *Tom Brown's School-*

days. The final description of the nineteen-year-old Tom as "captain of the eleven" which appears at the conclusion of Hughes's book has a very palpable intent on the reader's scale of moral values even though it is not couched in conventionally didactic or admonitory language. Townsend is really objecting less to the "didacticism" of *The Crofton Boys* than to the nature of the moral lesson being taught. Unlike Hughes, Martineau implicitly rejects the public school ethos of blind loyalty and team spirit as surpassing all other virtues in favor of a rather introspective individualism tempered by a sense of moral duty.

The Crofton Boys ends with Hugh traveling to India, "conscious that he went out well prepared for honourable duty." This may have a dated air for the modern reader, but the story itself is almost without a false note in its portrait of a child's psychological development. Hugh Procter is one of the first fully realized child characters in the history of literature for children. His desperate attempts to live up to his own conception of "a Crofton boy" despite the fact that he is both too young and too immature is convincingly shown. Most striking of all is Martineau's account of Hugh's daydreaming at his studies and his ineffectual attempts to make himself concentrate:

When his eyes were wandering, they observed boy after boy frowning over his dictionary, or repeating to himself, earnestly and without pause; and presently the business was done, and the learner at ease, feeling confident that he was ready to meet his master. After double the time had passed Hugh was still trying to get the meaning of his lesson into his head—going over the same words a dozen times, without gaining any notion of their meaning. . . . Sometimes he would begin saying his syntax in the middle of the night, fancying he was standing before Mr. Carnaby; and once he walked in his sleep as far as the head of the stairs, and then suddenly woke, and could not make out where he was.[17]

Hugh's painful transition from this dreamy abstractedness to a conscious taking of responsibility for himself and others through coming to terms with his lameness is the real subject of the novel. Not only is *The Crofton Boys* the first psychological novel in English for children, but it was not for another four or five decades until a substantial number of books for children with a comparable psychological depth and complexity would exist.

Of all Martineau's rarely read publications, it most deserves the attention of a modern audience.

The Power and Scope of her Fiction

Martineau estimated her own powers as a fiction writer very modestly. Despite the extraordinary popular success of her early illustrative and didactic tales, she claimed that her abilities as a writer of fiction were extremely limited, so that about ten years after the publication of *Illustrations of Political Economy* she "nearly ceased to write fiction, from simple inability to do it well" (3:462). In her assessment of her own career as a writer in the autobiographical sketch she intended to serve as her obituary she dismisses the significance of her fiction:

none of her novels or tales have, or ever had, in the eyes of good judges or in her own, any character of permanence. The artistic aim and qualifications were absent. She had no power of dramatic construction; nor the poetic inspiration on the one hand, nor critical cultivation on the other, without which no work of the imagination can be worthy to live. Two or three of her Political Economy Tales are, perhaps, her best achievements in fiction,—her doctrine furnishing the plot which she was unable to create, and the brevity of space duly restricting the indulgence in detail which injured her longer narratives, and at last warned her to leave off writing them. (3:462)

Although only such novels and tales as *Deerbrook, The Crofton Boys,* and *Feats on the Fiord* continue to be of interest, many of the features she isolates as flaws do not seem to the modern reader to be readily identifiable as serious defects. The lack of "critical cultivation," for example, and an "indulgence in detail" do not seem to be the central problems in her writing. She is closer to the mark in pointing to her lack of "power of dramatic construction." Except in some of the more tightly structured short tales, she seems to have experienced enormous difficulty with the action and plot of her narratives. Despite her extraordinarily systematic mind, she seems to have been totally bewildered by the prospect of having to construct a consistent plot. She readily admitted, for example, that *The Hour and the Man* had a hopelessly chaotic structure: "there are prominent

personages who have no necessary connexion whatever with
the story; and the personages fall out of sight, till at last, my
hero is alone in his dungeon, and the story ends with his solitary
death. I was not careless, nor unconscious of my inability. It
was inability, 'pure and simple' " (1:239). She goes so far as
to suggest that "creating a plot is a task above human faculties"
and that, as a power, it is akin to prophecy. She claims that
the only well-made plots in Dickens, Scott or other novelists
are "taken bodily from real life" (1:238). Her frank disbelief
in the possibility of generating action and plot as an organic
development of a fully imagined fictional world is an important
clue to the nature of her shortcomings as a novelist. The origin
of these difficulties lies in part in the literal-mindedness which
seems to have been an essential part of her personality, and
secondly in her approach to her "source material," which more
closely resembled the working method of the journalist who
consciously evaluates and incorporates deliberate research as
"background" to a story rather than the novelist who must fully
absorb background information and material before writing.
The journalist's method, necessitated by the exigencies of writing to a deadline, inevitably involves working with material
that is not thoroughly assimilated. Martineau's early experience
as a writer was one of working under constant pressure of dead-
lines, and it seems that she never revised her working method
to take advantage of a less pressing schedule.

  Although the vast majority of Martineau's fiction is of interest
to the modern reader because of the light it sheds on the history
of the period rather than because of its literary merit, her novels
and tales are chequered with episodes and passages which suggest that she narrowly missed becoming a Victorian novelist
of some significance. Certainly her main preoccupations as a
novelist and many of the characteristics of her fiction parallel
those of other nineteenth-century writers with more significant
achievements in fiction. Like Mrs. Gaskell, Dickens, and Charlotte Brontë she writes of unions, strikes, and the earlier machine-breaking phase of the industrial revolution. Like Scott,
Bulwer Lytton, and other popular novelists of the period, she
was attracted to historical subjects. The sense of place and the
precise observation of social life in a small community in *Deer-*

brook has much in common both with Gaskell's *Cranford* (1853) and the larger canvas of George Eliot's *Middlemarch* (1871–72).

Some of her preoccupations in her fiction are more idiosyncratic. She is fascinated by the precise details of domestic management and economy to a degree unusual even for a nineteenth-century novelist. In *Deerbrook,* when Margaret and Hester are shunned by the villagers, they are most distressed and inconvenienced by the reluctance of the village shopkeepers to serve them. Fascinated as always by the interaction between economic and social life, Martineau shows how Hester is intensely aware of the necessity of retaining the goodwill of shopkeepers in a small community: "She saw at once the difference in the relation between tradespeople and their customers in a large town like Birmingham, and in a village where there is but one baker, where the grocer and hatter are the same personage, and where you cannot fly from the butcher, be he ever so much your foe" (*D,* 197–98). In this and in numerous other similar episodes we see how Martineau's interest focuses on how social life is constructed and the way in which the shape of social interactions is largely predetermined by economic considerations.

In *Illustrations of Political Economy* she devotes long expository passages to the lengthy advice given by those who have learned sound domestic management to their less provident neighbors. In *Brooke and Brooke Farm* we are treated to pages of advice directed to an improvident cottager on how to drain land, make a compost heap, mend thatched roofs with furze, and so forth. Another cottager is warned about the way in which the tea-drinking habit can "ruin a very poor family."[18] Given her attraction to the problems of domestic management on very small means and resources, it is not surprising that Martineau, like other nineteenth-century writers of popular and children's literature, was drawn to the Robinson Crusoe theme in *Life in the Wilds,* one of the political economy tales, and in *The Settlers at Home.* The Crusoe theme inevitably appealed to Martineau and other like-minded writers of the period. It provided the opportunity to extrapolate lovingly on the minutiae of domestic management extolling the virtues of provident housekeeping.

It also offered the chance to promote the idea of self-reliance and, by implication, the whole political notion of laissez-faire capitalism.

Like other writers of fiction with an implicit or explicit didactic purpose, Martineau frequently uses the point of view of a naive or child character. This device was used ironically by other nineteenth-century novelists to show the moral failings or the folly of adult characters in a scene where the child's naive questions go inadvertently to the heart of the matter. The famous "What is money papa?" interchange between Paul Dombey and his father in *Dombey and Son*[19] is, perhaps, the most memorable example. For the most part, however, Martineau's naive child characters, like those of Mrs. Sherwood, seek and require instruction from adults, as, for example, the way in which the young girl in *Brooke and Brooke Farm* is persuaded by her "wise" father that the enclosure of "our pretty common" will eventually benefit everyone. Occasionally, even in her didactic fiction, Martineau is able to make use of a naive character's point of view to show the deficiencies of an apparently more sophisticated or more worldly view. An interesting example of this is in her tale *Demerara* where she uses the point of view of Alfred and Mary who return to their slave-owning father's plantation in Guiana after having been educated in England. Rather than lecturing the reader directly on the evils of slavery, Martineau has Alfred and Mary comment on the poverty-stricken and unthrifty appearance of everything they see on the slave-run estate compared with the prosperity of English farms run by wage-labor.

Perhaps Martineau's greatest weakness as a writer of fiction is her indulgence in exposition where dramatization would have served her purpose better. Although direct addresses to the reader occur frequently in nineteenth-century novels, in the hands of a George Eliot or a Mrs. Gaskell, they exist as an integral part of the novel's structure since they spring from a narrative voice that is a fully realized persona in the novel. Martineau, on the other hand, often volunteers what sounds like an idiosyncratic personal opinion on the action. While she does not indulge in frequent authorial interventions of the "Dear reader" variety, she has a tendency to tell rather than show what she wants the reader to know about the characters.

The action of the novels and tales only rarely fully embodies the ideas she wishes to incorporate and she is thus compelled to frame the action within passages of exposition to guarantee the reader's comprehension.

In *Deerbrook* some of the heavy-handedness of direct authorial comment is softened through her use of the governess, Maria Young, as a kind of alter-ego figure. Thus, many of her comments on education, on the grinding hard work of a governess's life, and some of the perspective on Deerbrook society are provided through Maria rather than through direct authorial intervention.

Nor are all her authorial interventions ill-conceived or poorly executed. Like George Eliot, Martineau is preoccupied, not only with external events of her characters' lives, but with their moment-to-moment mental life. For example, Hope's state of mind when he contemplates the prospect of the Ibbotson sisters leaving Deerbrook is one of perfect preparedness for falling in love:

It was already a heavy thought how dull Deerbrook would be without them. He was already unconsciously looking at every object in and around the familiar place with the eyes of the strangers, speculating on how the whole would appear to them. In short, his mind was full of them. There are, perhaps, none who do not know what this kind of impression is. All have felt it, at some time or other,—many have felt it often,—about strangers whom they have been predisposed to like, or with whom they have been struck at meeting. Nine times out of ten, perhaps, the impression is fleeting; and when it is gone, there is an unwillingness to return to it, from a sense of absurdity in having been so much interested about one who so soon became indifferent: but the fact is not the less real and general for this. When it happens between two young people who are previously fancy-free, and circumstances favour the impression till it sinks deeper than the fancy, it takes the name of love at first sight. Otherwise it passes away without a name, without a record:—for the hour it is a secret: in an after time it is forgotten. (*D,* 40)

Such a passage is not a piece of expendable authorial commentary, but is intrinsic to the total view of events provided in the novel. It sketches her characters' emotional susceptibility so that we are well-prepared for subsequent events, but, more important, her readers are reminded that we are ourselves all too familiar with such moments of susceptibility, and thus we are effectively prevented from condemning Hope's feelings as arbitrary or superficial.

Martineau's excessive reliance on exposition in her fiction may have arisen, in part, from her method of composition. She generally composed in her head and then committed herself to a single final copy, "thus saving an immense amount of time which I humbly think is wasted by other authors" (1:121). She evolved this method while attempting, early in her career, to write an historical novel but "found that it would not do to copy what I wrote; and here (at the outset of this novel) I discontinued the practice for ever . . . there was no use copying if I did not alter; and that if ever I did alter, I had to change back again; and I once for all, committed myself to a single copy" (1:121–22). Martineau was adamant that further revision would result only in "botching":

I have always made sure of what I meant to say, and then written it down without care or anxiety,—glancing at it again only to see if any words were omitted or repeated, and not altering a single phrase in a whole work. I mention this because I think I perceive that great mischief arises from the notion that botching in the second place will compensate for carelessness in the first. I think I perceive that confusion of thought, and cloudiness or affectation in style are produced or aggravated by faulty prepossessions in regard to the method of writing for the press. The mere saving of time and labour in my own case may be regarded as no inconsiderable addition to my term of life. (1:122)

Though there is always the salutory example of Ben Jonson's assertion that Shakespeare "never blotted a line," examining the manuscripts of major writers shows that the majority go through extensive revisions from the first draft to the final form. Even Dickens, who, like Harriet Martineau, wrote under the intense pressure of monthly publication, revised his manuscripts more and more extensively as his career developed.

Many of Martineau's tales show the effects, not so much of insufficient revision, but of a too deliberate use of background material and "setting." This is especially noticeable when she is writing of a place she has never visited, such as Guiana in *Demerara* or Norway in *Feats on the Fiord*. The reader has the

impression at times that passages of description of landscape
and local customs have been quickly adapted from a mélange
of encyclopedic sources rather than imaginatively realized. The
same sort of guide book approach frequently leads her into
generalizations about national or regional characteristics, which
prevents her from developing her characters as particular individuals. The individual characters in *Feats on the Fiord,* for example, remain rather indistinct for the first few chapters because
she is relying so heavily on generalizations about the food prefer-
ences, customs, and behavior of "all Norwegians." This overly
deliberate use of barely digested source material is absent from
the historical tales where Martineau is so familiar with the various historical accounts that she can draw on a rich fund of material rather than on scanty generalizations. Similarly, in a novel
with a contemporary English setting like *Deerbrook,* where she
relies on her own reminiscences and observation, she has no
need of formal descriptive passages outlining the setting or local
customs.

Martineau wrote in what many consider to be the Golden
Age of novel writing, and we are therefore compelled to judge
her fiction according to somewhat rigorous standards. The nineteenth-century novelists who are currently ranked highest in
the critical pantheon are probably those who, like Dickens, provide a huge cast of characters, or, like George Eliot or Mrs.
Gaskell, delineate a comprehensive relief map of the social landscape of the time. Martineau's fiction never aspires to this sort
of scope. The election scenes in Deerbrook might, at times,
be mistaken for the work of a writer like Mrs. Gaskell, but
the dramatic realization frequently falters and drops into crude
melodrama because she is so uncertain about the effect she is
creating. Martineau lacks the sustained fictional power required
to paint a large social canvas, nor, on the other hand, do we
find in her fiction the passionate intensity of a Charlotte or
Emily Brontë. Indeed Martineau, like many of her contemporaries, was strongly repulsed by Charlotte Brontë's most ambitious
novel, *Villette,* precisely because its intensity seemed to her to
come perilously close to morbidity. Her vision is essentially a
cool and rational one, but one that lacks the comprehensiveness
of a George Eliot or the intricate patterning of a Jane Austen.

Despite these shortcomings, her fiction is still of considerable interest to the serious student of nineteenth-century history and literature. While the modern general reader is usually impatient with obvious didactic or illustrative works, the serious student of the period will find a good deal to admire even in such works as *Illustrations of Political Economy*. *Deerbrook,* despite its unevenness, is of much greater interest and gives clear indications of a genuine and significant fictional gift. Martineau's only fully achieved works of fiction that can still be read for their strictly literary merit rather than their historical significance are *The Playfellow* stories and especially *The Crofton Boys,* which, alone among her fictional works, allows us to see the operation of a highly original intelligence on a vividly imagined fictional world.

Chapter Five

Critical Reputation

Martineau in the Eyes of Her Contemporaries

From the time she became a literary celebrity as the author of *Illustrations of Political Economy* until she established herself in comparative retirement at Ambleside, Martineau figures as a controversial subject in the letters and conversations of her contemporaries. Carlyle remarked in a letter to John Stuart Mill in December 1833 that "so much babbling pro and con has taken place about poor Miss M. that whenever I see her name I feel a kind of temptation to skip."[1] Certainly the plethora of references to her and to her writings in the correspondence of the second quarter of the nineteenth century suggests that she was a major celebrity as far as her contemporaries were concerned. Those, like J. S. Mill or the editors of the *Quarterly Review,* who actively disliked her were ready to suggest, however, that she herself was inclined to overrate her own notoriety.[2]

Yet a considerable celebrity she must have been if we can judge from the frequency with which her name occurs in the letters and journals of her contemporaries. The nineteenth-century Canadian humorist, Thomas Chandler Haliburton, was sufficiently certain that Martineau would be recognizable to his readers to make her the butt of his character Sam Slick in his sketch, "Travelling in America" (1849):

Year afore last, I met an English gal a-travellin' in a steamboat; she had a French name that I can't recollect, though I got it on the tip o' my tongue, too; you know who I mean—she wrote books on economy—not domestic economy, as gals ought, but on political economy, as gals oughtn't, for they don't know nothin' about it. She had a trumpet in her hand. Thinks I, who on airth is she a-goin' to hail, or is she a-goin' to try echoes on the river? I watched her for some time, and I found it was an ear trumpet. 'Well, well,' says I (to myself),

'that's onlike most English travellers anyway, for in a gineral way
they wear magnifyin' glasses, and do enlarge things so a body won't
know 'em ag'in when he sees 'em. Now, this gal wun't hear one
half that's said and will get that half wrong—' and so it turned out.[3]

Haliburton's joke at Martineau's expense is based less on her
individual foibles than on the way in which he (or at least his
persona, Sam Slick) thought that English travel writers were
apt to sum up their American experiences in vast generalizations
based on "a whole stock of notes. Spittin', gougin', lynchin',
burnin' alive, steamboats blowed up, snags, slavery, stealin'.
Texas, state prisons, men talk slow, women talk loud, both walk
fast, chat in steamboats and stagecoaches, anecdotes—and so
on. Then out comes a book."[4] Relying as it does on broad
humor, Haliburton's selection of Martineau as a prime target
among English travel writers does not suggest any real sense
of malice toward her, though it certainly underlines what a
widely known figure she had become.

Among the major figures of the nineteenth-century literary
scene, only J. S. Mill admits to an unalloyed dislike of Harriet
Martineau, regarding her as "narrow and matter-of-fact . . .
in the bad sense"[5] and thought that she was too ready to pass
judgment on others. Although she was too significant a journalist
to be denied access to the *Westminster Review,* Mill instructed
John Robinson to keep Martineau's contributions to the *Review*
to a bare minimum and he was insistent that he would not
himself deal with her directly.[6] He resisted any form of literary
association with her all his life and, as late as 1850, was outraged
to have his views on political economy coupled with those of
"a mere tyro like Harriet Martineau."[7]

Matthew Arnold seems to have had an essentially ambivalent
reaction to Martineau. On the one hand, his poem "Haworth
Churchyard," which compares her with Charlotte Brontë,
praises Martineau despite her unconventional religious views
because Arnold regarded her as a person "whose one effort
seems to have been to deal perfectly honestly with herself."
However, recalling his earlier poem in 1877, he was concerned
that he had overpraised her: "My first impression of her is, in
spite of her undeniable talent, energy and merit—what an unpleasant life and unpleasant nature!"[8]

Even George Eliot, who generally seems to have liked and admired Martineau, found some aspects of her nature unsympathetic, particularly disliking Martineau's carelessness in discussing other people's private lives: "Amongst her good qualities we certainly cannot reckon zeal for other people's reputation. She is sure to caricature any information for the amusement of the next person to whom she turns her ear trumpet."[9] In general, however, George Eliot tends to show a considerable regard for Martineau both as a person and as a writer even after she herself had forfeited Martineau's approval by living with George Henry Lewes. In a letter to her friends the Brays she says of Martineau: "After all she is a *trump*—the only English woman that possesses thoroughly the art of writing."[10] Even when they were no longer on good terms, George Eliot frequently asked her correspondents for news of Harriet Martineau and was anxious to write "an admiring appreciation" as an obituary if she outlived her.[11]

Her contemporaries responded variously to her mesmeric cure and the subsequent publicity she received. Elizabeth Barrett, herself an invalid at the time of her active correspondence with Martineau, was evidently timidly attracted to the idea of trying mesmerism herself and wondered wistfully whether Jane, Martineau's "apocalyptic housemaid," could tell her if her dog, Flush, had a soul.[12] She was annoyed however, by Martineau's request to her various correspondents that they destroy her letters and thought that it represented a wanton destruction of "the most vital part of biography."[13]

Martineau's agricultural activities at Ambleside also figure largely in discussions among her contemporaries, and even Matthew Arnold, who declared that he hardly knew a cow from a sheep, was inveigled into a tour of the establishment. Most of her literary correspondents seem to have viewed the Ambleside establishment with similar bewilderment, though only Robert Browning seems to have found it actually objectionable. In a rather rambling and confused letter to Elizabeth Barrett he comments censoriously that Martineau is wasting her talents by devoting time and energy to domestic and rural pursuits rather than devoting all her efforts to literary activities.[14]

Martineau's writings are frequently highly praised in the various correspondences of nineteenth-century literary figures. Eliza-

beth Barrett greatly admired all *The Playfellow* stories, while
George Eliot singled out *The Crofton Boys* for particular praise:
"What an exquisite little thing that is. . . . I have had some
delightful crying over it. There are two or three lines in that
that would feed one's soul for a month."[15] She was more critical
of the *History of the Thirty Years' Peace,* objecting to its "sentimental rhetorical style . . . which is fatiguing and not informative."[16]
Carlyle, though he liked Martineau personally, had mixed opinions about her work and was critical of *Deerbrook* as a "very
ligneous, very trivial-didactic" novel.[17] Nonetheless, he thought
highly of her gifts and capabilities. Even J. S. Mill found much
to admire in *Household Education* despite his dislike of almost
everything else Martineau wrote.[18]

An overview of the reactions of her contemporaries suggests
that, despite their considerable admiration for much of her writing, she was often puzzling and contradictory as a personality.
Thus, the typical reaction is one of admiration and affection
tinged with wariness, best expressed by Carlyle: "Good Harriet,
there is such a lively dispatch in her, such a sharp *needling* com-
pactness, one wishes her heartily well—at a distance."[19]

Martineau for Today

In many respects Martineau's modern reputation still carries
the residue of the ambivalent reactions her contemporaries had
toward her. On the one hand she was, in George Eliot's words
noted above, "a perfect *trump*" and "the only English woman
that possesses thoroughly the art of writing," and on the other
she was, as Mill asserted, "narrow" and difficult to like whole-
heartedly. Even the scope of her fame and influence was a subject
of heated disagreement among her contemporaries. Lord Brougham was irritated that the early efforts of his utilitarian Society
for the Diffusion of Useful Knowledge seemed quite overshad-
owed by the writings of Martineau, whom he described as
"a little deaf woman at Norwich."[20] Another utilitarian, Charles
Knight, who evidently felt more warmly toward Martineau, regarded her as very influential and reported on the way in which
her house in Fludyer Street "was frequented by crowds of visitors of rank and talent, eager to pay their homage to the young
authoress, whose little books went forth monthly in apparently

inexhaustible profusion."[21] Some years later, however, Robert Browning remarked sarcastically on Martineau's reluctance to come to London from Ambleside for fear of being *"mobbed to death,"*[22] evidently believing that Martineau seriously overrated her own notoriety.

These strong and contradictory responses she evoked from her contemporaries have continued to be reflected in the reactions of modern biographers who tend to find it difficult to strike a middle course between being sycophantic and hypercritical about their subject. Some biographers, like Fenwick Miller, have tended to be merely adulatory, while R. K. Webb goes to the opposite extreme and frequently gives the impression of heartily disliking his subject. Though intended for a general rather than a scholarly audience, the most balanced biography is probably Vera Wheatley's, while Valerie Kossew Pichanick's book provides the best view of Martineau in a historical context.

Until recently, the modern view of Harriet Martineau has tended to be of an interesting minor contemporary of the literary "greats" of the period, one whose sharp observations can offer insights into the lives and works of such figures as Carlyle, Dickens, or Browning. Most attention has also been devoted to her role as a political commentator rather than on her literary gifts, but there is some indication that this perspective may be in the process of shifting. As a woman making her living by writing in the nineteenth century and as an early feminist, Martineau is of considerable interest to modern feminist scholars. Consequently feminist publishers, such as Virago, have been instrumental in reissuing some of her long out-of-print works. Recently, too, literary scholars have been increasingly interested in autobiography as a literary genre, and this has resulted in a renewed interest in writers like Martineau whose autobiographies represent such a major part of their work. Prior to this recent resurgence of interest, virtually the only major critic who has accorded Martineau any real literary significance has been Kathleen Tillotson, whose *Novels of the Eighteen Forties* (1954) ranks *The Crofton Boys* with the fiction that Dickens and the Brontës produced during the same decade.

A major barrier to the modern reader's developing a clear sense of Martineau's significance in the context of her own time is the way in which her political views combined radicalism and conservatism in a way that has no counterpart in twentieth-century politics. On the one hand, her views are egalitarian and populist, but on the other, she preached a brand of economic individualism and laissez-faire capitalism that totally ignored the real plight of workers in the manufacturing industries.

Despite her difficult temperament and political views that are puzzling to readers who are not very familiar with nineteenth-century political and economic history, many of Martineau's writings, though not widely known, are still very accessible. One reason for this accessibility lies in her prose style. It is curiously "un-Victorian"—trenchant, direct, often almost conversational in its informality. It is practically free of the ornate convolutions that render so much Victorian prose impenetrable to the modern general reader. In part, this style arose from Martineau's method of composition, which involved careful mental formulation of her ideas and expression in a single, final draft.

Her work is accessible, too, because of her extraordinary sense of the memorable anecdote. Her travel books, her historical writings, her fiction, and most of all, her *Autobiography,* are constantly enlivened by the lightning sketches in which she shows us a character, a moment in time, a person's attitude, through a few deft strokes. When she sets out to describe a scene in a formal way with the object of making a deliberate record of events, as, for example, in her account of Queen Victoria's coronation in her *Autobiography,* her powers of description are impressive. In part, her ability to describe a scene so memorably arises, not so much from a gift for the apt descriptive phrase, but from her ability patiently to observe events. On occasion, particularly when she is describing a crowded or noisy scene, one has the sense that Martineau's deafness may have been a positive advantage in allowing her to pay undistracted attention to acutely observed visual impressions.

Martineau and the Art of Autobiography

Undoubtedly, the work that remains most attractive and interesting to modern readers is the *Autobiography.* Her contemporaries found it a somewhat shocking and distasteful document because of the way in which it portrayed her parents as cold and unloving and herself as the victim of their "want of tenderness." The reaction of many of the readers and reviewers of 1877 must be seen in the perspective of the mid-Victorian active promotion of the virtues of "hearth and home." The popular literature of the preceding two or three decades had sentimentalized the middle-class family to such an extent that Martineau's unfavorable portrait of her parents seemed both treacherous and morbid. The modern reader who is familiar with such later documents of the Victorian family as Samuel Butler's *The Way of All Flesh* and Edmund Gosse's *Father and Son* is less likely to find Martineau's portrait of her family either particularly unusual or self-indulgent.

In many respects Martineau's *Autobiography* is representative of the wave of interest in psychology and subjective experience, which was the motivating force behind many other important nineteenth-century works. It is this focus on the individual's early inner experiences that gives us the first book of Wordsworth's *The Prelude*, John Stuart Mill's *Autobiography*, the most absorbing parts of Mrs. Gaskell's *Life of Charlotte Brontë*, and, in fiction, the opening chapters of *David Copperfield* and *Great Expectations*. Martineau's *Autobiography*, idiosyncratic as it often is, has much in common with all such works. She is able to show the deeply felt quality of apparently trivial childhood experiences and to give a sense of her life unfolding in a coherent psychological pattern.

The work is full of sharp evocations of felt life like that of the two-year-old Harriet expressing a sense of "rapture" when touching a flat velvet button on a bonnet or the eight year old experiencing an epiphany characteristic of her generation on planting an apparently withered strawberry plant, finding that it revived with care and watering, and discovering in the experience "the first putting my hand in among the operations of Nature to modify them." Martineau evidently found the latter experience something of a watershed since she refers to it again in both *Health, Husbandry and Handicraft* and *Household Education*. The immediate experience of the adult Martineau is no less vividly rendered. We see her as a young woman trudging back to her relatives' house after yet another refusal from a publisher, "pretending to look at a cabbage bed, but saying to myself, as I stood with closed eyes, 'My book will do yet' "

(1:170). We read of her dash to Beachy Head to research the background for her political economy tale about smuggling, *The Loom and the Lugger,* writing her tale in the coach "on my knees all the way to London, in spite of the jolting," and arriving home to a pile of correspondence that had accumulated in her two days' absence, yet undaunted, despatching fourteen notes "and was at Lady S's by the time the clock struck six" (1:243).

Despite the fact that the literary tradition of autobiography stretches back to Saint Augustine's *Confessions* and beyond, compared with other literary genres, until quite recently, it has attracted only scanty critical analysis. In some respects this critical neglect springs from what might best be described as the established political economy of literary studies that structures itself principally around either period or genre study or the total oeuvre of particular writers within specific genres. Thus, it seems both convenient and natural to select for study such a body of work as eighteenth-century comedy, the nineteenth-century novel, Shakespeare's sonnets, Henry James's novels, Tennessee Williams's plays, and so on. It is relatively rare for writers to produce multiple autobiographies, thus the total autobiographical production of any given writer is likely to be a single work, which will tend to be studied, if at all, merely as a footnote to her or his works in some other genre. The most long-standing critical traditions, moreover, are those concerned with poetry and drama. Criticism of the novel can only date its respectability to the early decades of the twentieth century and the criticism of all other prose forms still tends to languish in limbo.

As a result of this relative critical neglect, conventional terminology and methods of classification are not yet firmly established for autobiography as they are for poetry or for drama. Such terms as "confessional" continue to be used in such diverse contexts and with such widely differing meanings that they are largely useless from a critical point of view. Northrop Frye has suggested that similar critical approaches to those used for the novel may be the most appropriate when dealing with autobiography: "Autobiography is a form which merges with the novel by a series of insensible gradations. Most autobiographies are inspired by a creative, and therefore fictional, impulse to select only those events and experiences in the writer's life that go to build up an integrated pattern. This pattern may be something larger than himself with which he has come to identify himself, or simply the coherence of his character and attitudes."[23]

Like the novel, then, the autobiography seeks to impose some sort of thematic order on the chaos of everyday existence. According to this definition, the autobiographer establishes or has already established some sort of definition of the self at the moment of writing and then proceeds to provide an account of how that self evolved as a result of particular experiences and influences.

In many respects, Martineau's autobiography is a clear example of the kind of organization and patterning that Frye describes. Not only does she provide a sharply defined self-portrait, confidently sketching in her amendments to what she perceived as public misconceptions about her opinions or activities, but she is also at pains to adhere meticulously to a strict chronology. The running heads of each page provide not only the calendar year, but also Martineau's own age at the time of the events described. The particular care devoted to placing events within such a precise chronological framework offers a clue to how Martineau perceived her task as autobiographer. She saw herself, as noted earlier, as a historian of her own times, documenting her impressions of major public events such as the passing of the New Poor Law or Queen Victoria's coronation. Against this backdrop of public experience she charts both her own psychic development from a repressed and troubled childhood to the achievement of a tranquil and philosophical state of mind and the progress of her career and rise in reputation as a writer.

The successful autobiography, however, must go far beyond the mere orderly assembly of events and memories stemming from a predetermined definition of the achieved self at the moment of writing. As with all literature of any real significance, the autobiography must itself be the means of discovering and exploring its subject. The autobiographer herself must understand her subject better and have explored her life more fully by the final chapter than at the outset. Roy Pascal describes this in his *Design and Truth in Autobiography:* "The life is represented in autobiography not as something established but as process: it is not simply the narrative of the voyage, but also the voyage itself. There must be in it a sense of discovery, and where this is wanting, and the autobiography appears as an exposition of something understood from the outset, we feel it a failure. . . ."[24] At first sight, Martineau's autobiography has the appearance of being more a "narrative of the voyage" than "the voyage itself." There are a number of set pieces that do not differ substantially from the versions of the same events already provided in her other works with an autobiographical component such as *Household Education, Society in America,* and *Eastern Travels.* In other respects, however, the reader frequently has the sense that the medium of autobiography has provided her with the means to explore some aspects of her life in ways not possible in other literary forms. For example, her account of the onset of her deafness and her analysis of the ways in which it influenced her subsequent development, as well as of her childhood troubles, has the hallmark of a sensitive area being honestly and painfully probed. She analyzes in some detail the way in which her deafness promoted what she saw as her restlessness and conscious search for diversion:

In my case, to be sure, the deficiency of three senses out of five renders the instance a very strong one: but the merely blind or deaf must feel something of the laboriousness of life which I have found it most difficult to deal with. People in general have only to sit in the midst of Nature, to be amused and *diverted* (in the strict sense of the word,— *distracted,* in the French sense) so as to find "change of work as good as rest": but I have had, for the main part of my life, to go in search of impressions and influences, as the alternative from abstract or unrelieved thought, in an intellectual view, and from brooding, in a moral view. (1:74–75)

If the view of "Nature" here is characteristic of the mid-nineteenth century, then the psychological analysis is strikingly modern. Martineau is perceptive about the ways in which those deprived of one or more senses find ordinary everyday life a continual process of work. The fatigue resulting from this labor, she suggests, frequently encourages "faults of temper, irritability or weakness of nerves, narrowness of mind, and imperfections of sympathy, in sufferers so worn with toil of body and mind as I, for one, have been" (1:75). This and other similar passages in the *Autobiography* are by no means the first occasion for Martineau to discuss the psychic and social cost of the loss or the absence of sensory perception, yet here, as elsewhere in her autobiography, her description is much more direct and personal, confronting her own immediate experience without the flimsy disguise of the third-person mask she adopts in *Household Education,* "Letter to the Deaf," or elsewhere in her journalism where she touches on her own experience.

All autobiographies are shaped not only by the events which make up the author's life, but also by the author's initial motive. Frequently the autobiographer approaches the subject with the intent of divulging information not previously made public. In modern popular autobiography this is often of the "now it can be told" variety which attracts readers by its aroma of scandal. In literary autobiography and in many autobiographies of public or political life, the project is prompted by the writer having outlived his or her contemporaries and therefore becoming able to speak freely about personalities and events without fear of either slighted feelings or of litigation.

Martineau embarked on her autobiography believing herself near death and, although she was only fifty-two, she had indeed outlived many of those who figure prominently in the anecdotes she relates. Brougham, Sydney Smith, and Wordsworth were all dead by the time she wrote her autobiography. Yet some of those whose actions had touched her life most crucially, like her brother James, were still alive, and she deals somewhat gingerly with the conflict that caused the final breach between herself and her brother.

Another common motive for autobiography is the impulse to set the record straight on matters or events in which the writer feels he or she has been publicly misrepresented. Martineau's autobiography seems to be impelled much more powerfully by this latter motivation than by the urge to divulge previously proscribed information. In one sense her autobiography seems to set out to modify the public perception of her as an opinionated self-publicist through providing a perspective on her personal reactions and inner experiences, thus humanizing what might otherwise have seemed a somewhat forbidding personality.

The most puzzling aspect of Martineau's motivation in writing her autobiography is that when her prediction about her immediate death proved unfounded and she lived on, albeit in increas-

ingly poor health, for over twenty years, she never modified
the summary of her life she had completed at the age of fifty-
two. The volumes remained bound and ready for distribution
and she entrusted the task of bringing the account up to date
in a third volume to her friend and admirer, Maria Weston
Chapman. Given Martineau's painstaking attempts to control
the content of the final assessment of her career, even through
such extreme means as providing her own obituary, allowing
Mrs. Chapman to assemble the final volume was a surprising
decision. It is particularly so since, despite her intense and often
cloying admiration for Martineau, Maria Chapman manages,
through sheer naïveté, to undermine some of Martineau's most
strongly held views. For instance, she expresses regret that Martineau did not die a Christian since this deprived her of "Unitarian
praises" at the time of her death! It may be that Martineau
overestimated the abilities her friend could bring to bear on
the task of final summing up but realized that Maria Chapman
was most unlikely to provide any harsh criticism in the posthumous volume. In her view this may have adequately acquitted
her autobiographical "duty."

Perhaps Martineau's principal contribution to the art of autobiography lies less in her exposition of her own psychic or philosophical development as in her gift for swiftly conveying sharp
and sometimes comic impressions of a character or an event.
Wordsworth's niggardliness in providing for his guests, Brougham's discomfort with intellectual women, the social perils of
becoming a literary "lion" are deftly and economically sketched
through her gift for accurately recording the telling remark
or the revealing anecdote. Even when she describes some of
the stormier passages of her own life she retains much of the
same comic detachment, so that her mother's domineering personality, the threats on her life from slave owners during her
American travels, and the public antagonism that resulted from
her *Letters on Mesmerism* and the *Letters on the Laws and Nature
of Man's Development* are all assessed with the same cool ironic
gaze and with a superb economy of language.

Chapter Six

Conclusion

The main fascination of the account of her career Martineau offers in her *Autobiography* is that it is at the same time both unique and typical. That Martineau, as a young woman from a provincial town who was almost totally deaf, could become a literary "lion" in the London of the 1830s tells us that she was, of course, a rather extraordinary woman. It also tells us something about the way in which the development of a mass readership was opening the literary world, if not to all comers, then at least to exceptional outsiders like Martineau, Dickens, and later, Charlotte Brontë.

Other aspects of Martineau's career are also characteristically Victorian. She was, for instance, one of the many notable nineteenth-century figures who were invalids for a long period. The phenomenon of invalidism in the nineteenth century remains an intriguing and unsolved problem for students of nineteenth-century literature and history. An extraordinary number of individuals, the large majority of them women, like Martineau herself, Elizabeth Barrett, and Florence Nightingale, spent many years in retirement because of apparently extremely serious, but not fatal, illnesses. Cecil Woodham-Smith has suggested in her life of Florence Nightingale[1] that, in Nightingale's case at any rate, invalidism was a convenient way of avoiding trivial domestic and social responsibilities and allowing herself time to pursue her work. R. K. Webb[2] has suggested, I believe quite wrongly, that Martineau's illness was strictly psychosomatic. Ample evidence exists to show that her symptoms had a physiological origin. Nevertheless, the status of invalid was a socially recognized one for Victorian women and one that enabled Martineau to pursue an important part of her literary career relatively undisturbed.

Like other major Victorian figures, Martineau spent many years of her life wrestling with religious doubts until she reached a resolution of the paradoxes she saw in Christianity through the necessarian solution. Her account of her inner struggles about religion in the *Autobiography* probably understates the personal anguish involved because she is so intent on showing how effectively necessarianism resolved her doubts. However, her account of the opposition she encountered from her family and from acquaintances and neighbors when she finally made public her disavowal of Christian belief in the *Letters on the Laws of Man's Nature and Development* provides a valuable insight into the intensity of feeling that attended Victorian religious debate and which was to burst forth so dramatically in the late Victorian controversy over evolution.

Martineau's contribution to the popular Victorian genre of travel writing is an unusual and an important one. Before extensive travel was available to any but a privileged few and before photography was widespread, travel books tended to stress the most exotic aspects of the locations described and to ignore anything that smacked of the homespun or the mundane. This hyperbolic tendency is reflected in the work of Victorian visual artists like Edward Lear who traveled abroad to make sketches of spectacular scenery which were then published as books of "views." The sketches and paintings of Lear and other traveling artists tended to emphasize everything that was least familiar about the scene being portrayed. Huge waterfalls, colossal mountain peaks, and gigantic cataracts became the stock-in-trade for the artists catering to English taste, which, as a result of the influence of the romantic movement, was finding English pastoral scenery altogether too tame. Travel writers of the period similarly emphasize the exotic aspects of scenery and customs and they stress to their readers that the inhabitants of other countries are irreconcilably different and strange. Martineau's travel writings differ from those of her contemporaries in that she is only rarely interested in the grand spectacle or the exotic custom but is constantly fascinated by the familiar and the domestic. Thus an anecdote about a woman and her cow at Niagara Falls seems more important than the Falls themselves, and her reflections about her early Bible-reading experiences take precedence over the stark desert scenery in *Eastern Life*. Similarly, she is constantly at pains to point out the resemblance between familiar experiences at home and those of the traveler. For example, when she witnesses a demonstration by a "magician" in Cairo who had greatly impressed other English travelers she asks one of her friends "to tell the man that I had seen curious things done in England, and knew the truth of such *clairvoyance* as he professed to show" (*E, 256*). Always in her travels, she is interested above all in how society works, but especially in how the larger society is reflected in the minutiae of domestic life. Her observations on slavery in America, therefore, focus not so much on the moral issue but rather on how its shortcomings as an institution affected the day-to-day operation of domestic economy.

Martineau undoubtedly saw herself from the beginning of her literary career as a teacher. At the outset she saw her task as teaching the principles of political economy to the British nation through the contrived parables of her *Illustrations of Political Economy.* Later, her audience extended to the international English-speaking world and the scope of her subject broadened to become more informal in tone and arising essentially from her own experiences of domestic life and management. In this respect she very much resembles William Cobbett, though her manner of presenting her views is rather less choleric. Like Cobbett, her approach to her subject is engaging because the advice she offers her readers is presented, not in a high-handed or patronizing manner, but from the point of view of one who is herself closely involved in the activities she recommends.

Her popular educative works also illustrate for us the way in which a mass reading public was emerging in the first half of the nineteenth century. The success of such works as *Illustrations of Political Economy* and *Household Education* suggests that the emerging reading public had an intense interest in "self-improvement" and used private reading as a means to that end.

Martineau's estimate of her own powers as a writer of fiction was a modest one. She concluded, as noted earlier, that none of her novels or tales could be said to "have any character of permanency." Although her fiction is flawed in several ways, it is, however, quite unjust to dismiss it as merely ephemeral.

Undoubtedly, the most serious shortcoming was her apparent inability to create a fully imagined world from which plot and action could develop naturally and inevitably without being artificially contrived. She found it hard to believe that other writers could actually create plots with ease and told herself that the plots of other novelists must have been taken wholesale from real life. This failing seems to have arisen from her essential literal-mindedness, which served her well in her various essays and *The History of the Thirty Years' Peace* but which was a serious handicap for a novelist.

Despite her limitations, there is much of value even in an uneven novel like *Deerbrook*. Minor characters like Maria Young and Sophia Grey are drawn with considerable sensitivity. She is particularly skillful in her delineation of the social pressures and tensions of provincial life. *Deerbrook* is also of significant historical value because of the remarkable portrait it provides of early Victorian electioneering.

Although Martineau herself did not seem to regard them as a particularly important achievement, the four children's tales published in *The Playfellow* are likely to continue to be her best-known work. There is a fresh, unforced quality about all four tales which makes them most unusual considering that a specific literature for children had only just begun to emerge at the time they were written. Of the four tales, *The Crofton Boys,* though not as well-known as *Feats on the Fiord,* is an outstanding exploration of a child's psychological development.

Martineau's literary and personal career was, as she herself recognized, "a somewhat remarkable one." She considered herself only moderately talented, and certainly a reading of her works does not reveal an impressive imaginative genius of the order of Dickens or the Brontës. Her gift was, in many respects, a more taxing and demanding one, for she set herself the task of recording the sights, the events, and the people of her own time with a steady, careful, and patient eye.

Notes and References

Preface

1. R. K. Webb, *Harriet Martineau: A Radical Victorian* (London, 1960).
2. Vera Wheatley, *The Life and Work of Harriet Martineau* (London, 1957).
3. Valerie K. Pichanick, *Harriet Martineau: The Woman and Her Work 1802–76* (Ann Arbor, 1980), 89.
4. Richard D. Altick, *The English Common Reader: A Social History of the Mass Reading Public 1800–1900* (Chicago, 1957).

Chapter One

1. *Harriet Martineau's Autobiography: With Memorials by Maria Weston Chapman,* 3 vols. (London, 1877), 1:180; hereafter cited in the text.
2. Jane Marcet, *Conversations on Political Economy, in which the elements of that science are familiarly explained* (London: Longman, Hurst, Rees, Orme and Brown, 1816).
3. V. de Sola Pinto, ed., *Byron's Poems* (London: J. M. Dent, 1963), 1:217.
4. "Miss Martineau's Monthly Novels," *Quarterly Review* 49 (1833):136.
5. Ibid., 151.
6. Cecil Woodham-Smith, *Florence Nightingale 1820–1910* (London: Constable, 1950), 302–5.
7. Pichanick, *Harriet Martineau,* 89.
8. Thomas Greenhow, *A Medical Report of the Case of Miss H—— M——,* London: Samuel Highley, 1845.
9. Webb, *Harriet Martineau,* 226–53.
10. *Weekly Dispatch* (n.d.) quoted in Pichanick, *Harriet Martineau,* 187.
11. Gordon S. Haight, ed., *The George Eliot Letters* (New Haven: Yale University Press, 1954), 1:364, 6:371.
12. Quoted in Pichanick, *Harriet Martineau,* 189.
13. Woodham-Smith, *Florence Nightingale,* 395.
14. Quoted in Wheatley, *Life and Work,* 376.

Chapter Two

1. Jane Louise Mesick, *The English Traveler in America 1785–1835* (New York: Columbia University Press, 1922), 12.
2. *Society in America,* 3 vols. (London, 1837), 16; hereafter cited in the text as *S.*
3. *Retrospect of Western Travel,* 3 vols. (London, 1838), 1:44; hereafter cited in the text as *R.*
4. *Eastern Life, Present and Past,* 3 vols. (London, 1848), 299; hereafter cited in the text as *E.*
5. Elaine Showalter, *A Literature of Their Own: British Women Novelists from Bronte to Lessing* (Princeton: Princeton University Press, 1977), has a useful account of the social milieu of nineteenth-century women writers. See especially 37–72.

Chapter Three

1. William Cobbett, *Cottage Economy: containing information relative to the brewing of Beer, making of Bread, keeping of Cows, Pigs, Bees, Ewes, Goats, Poultry and Rabbits, and relative to other matters deemed useful in the conducting of the affairs of a Labourer's Family* (London, 1821–22); it was issued in monthly parts.
2. London: Bradbury and Evans, 1861, The Library of Congress incorrectly catalogs *Our Farm of Four Acres* as being by Martineau herself.
3. Published in London, entitled the *Penny Magazine of the Society for the Diffusion of Useful Knowledge* from 1832 to 1846; in 1846 it was called *Knight's Penny Magazine.*
4. *Health, Husbandry and Handicraft* (London, 1861), vi; hereafter cited in the text as *H.*
5. Jean Jacques Rousseau, *Emile, ou De l'education* (Paris: Duchesne, 1762).
6. *Household Education* (London, 1849), 11; hereafter cited in the text as *HE.*
7. *Our Farm of Two Acres* (New York: Bunce & Huntingdon, 1865).
8. *Brooke and Brooke Farm* (Boston: Leonard C. Bowles, 1832).
9. Auguste Comte, *Cours de philosophie positive,* 6 vols. (Paris: Bachelier, 1830–42).
10. *The Positive Philosophy of Auguste Comte freely translated and condensed* (New York: Calvin Blanchard, 1855), 9.
11. George Henry Lewes, *Biographical History of Philosophy* (London: Charles Knight, 1845–46), published weekly.

12. Herbert Spencer, *Social Statics: or, The Conditions essential to human happiness specified and the first of them developed* (London: John Chapman, 1851).

13. Webb, *Harriet Martineau*, 307–9.

14. *The History of England during the Thirty Years' Peace 1816–46*, 2 vols. (London, 1849).

15. *British Rule in India* (London, 1857).

16. *History of the Peace* 2:240.

17. Elie Halevy, *Histoire du peuple anglais au XIXe siecle* (Paris: Hachette, 1913).

18. *British Rule in India*, 2.

19. *Biographical Sketches* (London: Macmillan, 1869); hereafter cited in the text as *B.*

20. *Household Words* 9 (1854):317–20.

21. Ibid., 10 (1854):421–25.

22. Ibid., 9 (1854):197–98.

23. Ibid., 11 (1855):529–39, 565–73, 587–99, 609–19.

24. Manchester: National Association of Factory Occupiers, 1855.

25. Charles Dickens, "Our Wicked Mis-statements," *Household Words* 13 (1856):13–19.

26. Letter to W. H. Wills, January 1856; quoted in Harry Stone, *Charles Dickens' Uncollected Writings from Household Words 1850–1859* (Bloomington: Indiana University Press, 1968), 2:550.

27. *The Playfellow* (London, 1841).

28. *Deerbrook,* 3 vols. (London, 1839); hereafter cited in the text as *D.*

29. "Letter to the Deaf," *Tait's Edinburgh Magazine,* 1834, 174–79.

30. *Life in the Sickroom* (London, 1844).

31. "Letter to the Deaf," 174.

32. Ibid.

33. Ibid., 174–75.

34. Ibid., 175.

35. *Life in the Sickroom,* 49–50.

36. George Eliot, *Middlemarch: A Study of Provincial Life* (Edinburgh: William Blackwood, 1891), 571.

Chapter Four

1. Wheatley, *Life and Work,* 96.

2. *Norwich Mercury;* quoted in preliminary pages (unpaginated) of *Demerara* (Boston: Leonard C. Bowles, 1832).

3. *Poor Man's Guardian,* 7 January 1832; quoted in Webb, *Harriet Martineau,* 103–4.
4. *A Manchester Strike* (Boston: Leonard C. Bowles, 1832), 177.
5. *Demerara,* 120.
6. *Brooke and Brooke Farm,* 117–19.
7. Thomas Hutchinson, ed., *The Poetical Works of Wordsworth* (London: Oxford University Press, 1904), 242.
8. Gordon S. Haight, ed., *The George Eliot Letters,* (New Haven: Yale University Press, 1954), 1:192.
9. Kathleen Tillotson, *The Novels of the Eighteen Forties* (Oxford: Clarendon Press, 1954), 5, 549.
10. *The Playfellow* (London: George Routledge, 1856), 243.
11. *Quarterly Review* 74 (1844):21.
12. *The Playfellow,* 401.
13. Ibid., 440.
14. Ibid., 485.
15. Ibid., 498.
16. John R. Townsend, *Written For Children* (London: Kestrel Books, 1965), 112.
17. *The Playfellow,* 423.
18. *Brooke and Brooke Farm,* 126.
19. Charles Dickens, *Dombey and Son* (London: Oxford University Press, 1950), 52.

Chapter Five

1. Charles Richard Sanders and Kenneth J. Fielding, eds., *The Collected Letters of Thomas and Jane Welsh Carlyle* (Durham: Duke University Press, 1977), 7:66.
2. *Quarterly Review* 143 (1877):484. See also Elvan Kintner, ed., *The Letters of Robert Browning and Elizabeth Barrett Barrett 1845–1846* (Cambridge: Belknap Press, 1969), 2:993.
3. Walter Avis and R. Watters, eds., *The Sam Slick Anthology* (Toronto: Clarke Irwin, 1969), 62.
4. Ibid., 61.
5. Francis E. Mineka, ed., *The Collected Works of John Stuart Mill* (Toronto: University of Toronto Press, 1963), 12:140.
6. Ibid., 12:342.
7. Ibid., 14:53.
8. Howard Foster Lowry, ed., *The Letters of Matthew Arnold and Arthur Hugh Clough* (New York: Russell & Russell, 1932), 131.
9. *The George Eliot Letters,* 2:180.
10. Ibid., 2:32.

11. Ibid., 2:258.

12. Frederic G. Kenyon, ed., *The Letters of Elizabeth Barrett Browning* (New York: Macmillan, 1897), 1:212.

13. *The Letters of Robert Browning and Elizabeth Barrett Barrett,* 1:469.

14. Ibid., 1:463–66.

15. *The George Eliot Letters,* 1:192.

16. Ibid., 2:430.

17. Alexander Carlyle, ed., *New Letters of Thomas Carlyle* (London: Bodley Head, 1904), 2:159.

18. *Collected Works of John Stuart Mill,* 16:1469.

19. *New Letters of Thomas Carlyle,* 1:159.

20. Quoted in Wheatley, *Life and Work,* 85.

21. Charles Knight, *Passages of a Working Life During Half a Century,* 3 vols (London: Bradbury & Evans, 1864), 2:315.

22. *The Letters of Robert Browning and Elizabeth Barrett Barrett,* 2:997.

23. Northrop Frye, *Anatomy of Criticism* (Princeton: Princeton University Press, 1957), 307.

24. Roy Pascal, *Design and Truth in Autobiography* (Cambridge: Harvard University Press, 1960), 82.

Chapter Six

1. Woodham-Smith, *Florence Nightingale,* 302–5.

2. Webb, *Harriet Martineau,* 226–53.

Selected Bibliography

PRIMARY SOURCES

The first editions of many of Martineau's works are now frequently extremely difficult to obtain. Consequently, the editions referred to in the text are the earliest editions that are currently readily available in North America. The editions cited in the bibliography are all first editions.

1. Autobiographical and Biographical Writings
Biographical Sketches. London: Macmillan and Co., 1869.
Harriet Martineau's Autobiography: With Memorials by Maria Weston Chapman. 3 vols. London: Smith, Elder and Co., 1877.

2. Popular Educative Literature
How to Observe: Morals and Manners. London: Charles Knight, 1838.
Guide to Service. London: Charles Knight, 1841
Life in the Sickroom: Essays by an Invalid. London: Edward Moxon, 1844.
Household Education. London: Edward Moxon, 1849.
Two Letters on Cow Keeping . . . Addressed to the Governor of the Guiltcross Union Workhouse. London: Charles Gilpin, 1850.
Health, Husbandry and Handicraft. London: Bradbury & Evans, 1861.

3. Historical and Political Writings
The Martyr Age in the United States. New York: S. W. Benedict, 1839. Reprinted from the *London and Westminster Review.*
History of England During the Thirty Years' Peace 1816–46. 2 vols. London: Charles Knight, 1849.
Introduction to the History of the Peace from 1800 to 1815. London: Charles Knight, 1851.
The Factory Controversy: A Warning Against Meddling Legislation. Manchester: National Association of Factory Occupiers, 1855.
A History of the American Compromises. London: John Chapman, 1856. Reprinted, with additions from the *Daily News.*
The "Manifest Destiny" of the American Union. New York: American

Anti-Slavery Society, 1857. Reprinted from the *Westminster Review.*

British Rule in India: A Historical Sketch. London: Smith, Elder and Co., 1857.

Suggestions Towards the Future Government of India. London: Smith, Elder and Co., 1858.

England and Her Soldiers. London: Smith, Elder and Co., 1859.

4. Fiction

Principle and Practice; or, the Orphan Family: A Tale. London: Houlston, 1827.

The Turn Out; or, Patience the Best Policy. London: Houlston and Son, 1829.

Five Years of Youth; or, Sense and Sentiment! A Tale. London: Harvey and Darton, 1831.

Illustrations of Political Economy. 9 vols. London: Charles Fox, 1834. First appeared as monthly numbers (London: Charles Fox, 1832).

Poor Laws and Paupers. 4 vols. London: Charles Fox, 1833.

Christmas Day; or, The Friends. London: Houlston, 1834.

Illustrations of Taxation. 4 vols. London: Charles Fox, 1834.

Deerbrook. 3 vols. London: Edward Moxon, 1839.

The Playfellow. 4 vols. London: Charles Knight, 1841.

The Hour and the Man. 3 vols. London: Edward Moxon, 1841.

Dawn Island. Manchester: J. Gadsby, 1845.

Forest and Game Law Tales. 3 vols. London: Edward Moxon, 1845–46.

The Billow and the Rock. London: Charles Knight, 1846.

5. Travel Writings

Society in America. 3 vols. London: Saunders & Otley, 1837.

Retrospect of Western Travel. 3 vols. London: Saunders & Otley, 1838.

Eastern Life, Present and Past. 3 vols. London: Edward Moxon, 1848.

Guide to Windermere, with Tours to the Neighbouring Lakes and Other Interesting Places. . . . Windermere: John Garnett, 1854.

A Complete Guide to the English Lakes. Windermere: John Garnett, 1855.

Guide to Keswick and its environs. Windermere: John Garnett, 1857.

6. Religious and Philosophical Writings

Devotional Exercises consisting of Reflections and Prayers for the use of Young Persons: to which is added a Treatise on the Lord's Supper. By a Lady. London: Rowland Hunter, 1823.

Addresses with Prayers and Original Hymns for the use of Families. . . . By a Lady. London: Rowland Hunter, 1826.

Traditions of Palestine. London: Longman, Rees, Orme Brown &
    Greene, 1830.
The Essential Faith of the Universal Church: Deduced from the Sacred Records.
    London: Unitarian Society, 1831.
*The Faith as unfolded by Many Prophets: An Essay . . . Issued by the British
    and Foreign Unitarian Association and addressed to the Disciples of
    Mohammed.* London: Unitarian Society, 1832.
*Providence as manifested through Israel: An Essay . . . Issued by the British
    and Foreign Unitarian Association and addressed to the Jews.* London:
    Unitarian Society, 1832.
Letters on Mesmerism. London: Edward Moxon, 1845.
Letters on the Laws of Man's Nature and Development. London: John
    Chapman, 1851. With Henry Atkinson.
The Positive Philosophy of Auguste Comte. 2 vols. London: John Chapman,
    1853. Martineau translated and condensed Comte's original work.

SECONDARY SOURCES

1. Bibliography

The Cambridge Bibliography of English Literature, edited by F. W. Bate-
son, contains a partial bibliography. Joseph B. Rivin, "Harriet Martineau: A Bibliography of her Separately Printed Works" (*Bulletin of
the New York Public Library* 50 [1947]), provides a complete bibliography of books and articles but not of her extensive publications in
periodicals. *The Wellesley Index of Periodicals 1824–1900* documents
Martineau's contributions to the *Cornhill Magazine,* the *Edinburgh Review,* the *Quarterly Review,* the *London and Westminster Review,* and
the *Westminster Review.*

2. Criticism and Biography

The biographies and published letters of all of the following of
Martineau's contemporaries are an abundant source of biographical
information to add to and modify Martineau's own account in her
autobiography: Matthew Arnold, Charlotte Brontë, Elizabeth Barrett
and Robert Browning, Jane Welsh and Thomas Carlyle, George Eliot,
James Martineau, and John Stuart Mill.

Altick, Richard D. *The English Common Reader: A Social History of
    the Mass Reading Public 1800-1900.* Chicago: University of Chi-
    cago Press, 1957. A vital source of information for understanding
    the social context of nineteenth-century popular literature.
"Auguste Comte: A Messiah for the Age of Positivism." *Times Literary*

Supplement 83 (1974):1–2. A useful assessment of the contemporary response to Comte.

Bosanquet, Theodora. *Harriet Martineau: An Essay in Comprehension.* London: Etchels & H. Macdonald, 1927. The earliest attempt to evaluate Martineau's career critically, but adds little to the information contained in the *Autobiography.*

Fay, C. R. "Economics in a Novel." *Dalhousie Review* 12 (1932):180–81. Extremely brief but cogent summary of Martineau's popularization of Malthus's views in her *Illustrations of Political Economy.*

Kaplan, F. "Mesmeric Mania: The Early Victorians and Animal Magnetism." *Journal of the History of Ideas* 35 (1974):691–702. Provides important background to Victorian attitudes toward mesmerism.

Knight, Charles. *Passages of a Working Life During Half a Century.* London: Bradbury & Evans, 1864. Gives a unique insight from the point of view of a publisher of popular literature on literary life in early Victorian London.

Martin, Robert B. "Charlotte Brontë and Harriet Martineau." *Nineteenth Century Fiction* 7 (1952):198–201. An account of the meeting between Charlotte Brontë and Martineau quoting in full a previously unpublished letter by Martineau's hostess that describes the event.

Miller, F. Fenwick. *Harriet Martineau.* London: W. H. Allen, 1889. An adulatory biography somewhat in the same vein as Maria Weston Chapman's "Memorial" in volume 3 of the *Autobiography.*

Nevill, John Cranstoun. *Harriet Martineau.* London: Frederick Muller, 1943. A readable popular biography that serves as a reasonable introduction to Martineau's life and work for the general reader.

Oliphant, M. O. "Harriet Martineau." *Blackwoods Magazine* 84 (1877):472–96. A lengthy review of the *Autobiography* raising many of the objections of "morbidity" and self-centeredness that characterized critical reactions to the book.

Pichanick, Valerie Kossew. *Harriet Martineau: The Woman and Her Work 1802–76.* Ann Arbor: University of Michigan Press, 1980. A soundly researched biography that concerns itself with Martineau's significance as a historical figure but sheds little insight on her literary significance.

————. "An Abominable Submission: Harriet Martineau's Views on the Role and Place of Women." *Women's Studies* 5 (1977):13–32. A valuable summary of Martineau's views on feminism that effectively counters some of R. K. Webb's unsoundly based arguments.

Pope-Hennessy, Una. *Three English Women in America.* London: Benn,

1929. An account of the American experiences of Martineau, Fanny Trollope, and Fanny Kemble.

Tillotson, Kathleen. *The Novels of the Eighteen Forties.* Oxford: Clarendon Press, 1954. One of the best books on Victorian fiction ever written, showing the common tradition that produced the once popular and now forgotten works along with those that have acquired the status of "classics." Tillotson is one of the few major critics to rank *The Crofton Boys* with the major fiction of the period.

Webb, R. K. *Harriet Martineau: A Radical Victorian.* London: Heinemann, 1960. An assessment of Martineau and her career in a political and historical rather than a literary context. Includes some valuable material unavailable elsewhere but takes an oddly antagonistic approach to Martineau herself, which distorts the interpretation.

Wheatley, Vera. *The Life and Work of Harriet Martineau.* London: Secker & Warburg, 1957. A well-researched general biography that is marred by an inappropriate prose style. Since it is directed at a general rather than a scholarly audience, it is insufficiently referenced for scholarly purposes.

Index

143